Web Content Management

A Collaborative Approach

Russell Nakano

Addison-Wesley

Boston • San Francisco • New York • Toronto • Montreal
London • Munich • Paris • Madrid
Capetown • Sydney • Tokyo • Singapore • Mexico City

Many of the designations used by manufacturers and sellers to distinguish their products are claimed as trademarks. Where those designations appear in this book, and Addison-Wesley was aware of a trademark claim, the designations have been printed with initial capital letters or in all capitals.

The author and publisher have taken care in the preparation of this book, but make no expressed or implied warranty of any kind and assume no responsibility for errors or omissions. No liability is assumed for incidental or consequential damages in connection with or arising out of the use of the information or programs contained herein.

The publisher offers discounts on this book when ordered in quantity for special sales. For more information, please contact:

Pearson Education Corporate Sales Division
201 W. 103rd Street
Indianapolis, IN 46290
(800) 428-5331
corpsales@pearsoned.com

Visit AW on the Web: www.aw.com/cseng/

Library of Congress Cataloging-in-Publication Data

Nakano, Russell.
  Web content management : a collaborative approach / Russell Nakano.
     p. cm.
  Includes bibliographical references and index.
  ISBN 0-201-65782-1 (alk. paper)
    1. Web sites--Management. I. Title.

 TK5105.888 .N35 2001
 005.2'76--dc21   2001041318

For information on obtaining permission for use of material from this work, please submit a written request to:

Pearson Education, Inc.
Rights and Contracts Department
75 Arlington Street, Suite 300
Boston, MA 02116
Fax: (617) 848-7047

Text printed on recycled and acid-free paper.

 ISBN 0201657821

 2 3 4 5 6 7 DOC 04 03 02 01

 2nd Printing   December 2001

This book is dedicated to Mira, Lisa, and Gail, who encouraged me and endured my constant preoccupation throughout this project.

CONTENTS

FOREWORD

Before the web began it's meteoric ascent in the mid-90s, it was easy to find naysayers around every corner. But by 1996, with the Internet frenzy in full swing, one of my ever-optimistic managers was continually comparing Silicon Valley to "Paris in the '20s." Today, with the demise of the dot-bombs a not-so-distant memory, E*trade junkies mingle at cocktail parties swearing they "told you the bubble was going to burst."

Over the past five or six years, an underworld of individuals has wielded enormous influence over the manner in which the web has taken root in *Fortune* 500 companies. These members of the digerati are not gadfly marketers, nor the privacy experts du jour. Rather, they are people who have focused their professional careers on growing the web within their respective corporate cultures. They are web practitioners, and Russell Nakano is one of the best in the business. This book is a testament to his deep experience and unparalleled expertise in the field.

Those of you with web production experience already know the vital contribution that content managers make to a web team. For others who are new to content management, this book provides a solid foundation for how to plan (and re-plan) a web site that lives...rather than one that requires harrowing cycles of resuscitation, and gobs of "look-and-feel" money.

In 1996, I started consulting with Xerox. This was at a time when the company's web site was migrating from its prior function, as the Palo Alto Research Center's digital "front door," to its new role as the company's official corporate presence. The project was immense, and involved more humans than any other migration I had witnessed to date. My first few months at Xerox were spent with two colleagues and a manager, the three of us executing a range of keyboard heroics, making countless "stakeholder" phone calls, and enduring some very funny sessions with a well-known design agency.

The agency—never having dealt with an entity as overwhelming as xerox.com—limited its deliverables to graphical assets. What was missing was a sustainable method by which we could manage the site over the long term. Customer inquiries typically elicited fait-accompli storyboard presentations to various stakeholder groups, inevitably spiraling downward into heated discussions about appropriate color palettes.

In those days, building web sites simply didn't follow the rigors of new-product introductions, nor was there ever talk of any formal, post-launch support process. In one memorable instance, I can recall our long-awaited, web-based 1996 Olympics Guide arriving just as the last medals were being awarded.

Realizing that agencies were not a viable content source, I proposed a distributed authorship model that called on the corporation's employees to contribute to the site on a day-in, day-out basis. The outcome was a guidelines and standards manual I authored, with the help of two colleagues. The guidelines initially met with some resistance from a small group of xerox.com early-adopters, who, until that time, had published as they saw fit. However, the model had a liberating effect on the rest of the corporation, in that it enabled Xerox stakeholders to publish "compliant" content for their customers. Coupled with the rollout of our first content management system, the age of distributed authorship, templates, and the "emergency push" began.

Russell includes many illustrative, colorful scenarios like this one in his book. Through these mini case studies, he helps show why a content management system should be focused on the people it's intended to include: the stakeholders across the enterprise and the individuals who make up corporate web organizations.

I'm sure Russell would agree that all great web sites have content machinations in place that work to support content contributors, who, in turn, look out for the customers' needs. In other words, great web sites may be primed by talented agencies. But such sites only survive past the first day if the supporting content flows from within the enterprise.

Getting that to happen depends on change process management, as well as pushing the boundaries of organizational behavior. I remember converting critical stakeholders by inviting them to "join the party." Ultimately, the idea of providing canned, "aesthetic" templates was reluctantly accepted because of the need for publishing flexibility. Stakeholders simply realized it was a more efficient and better way to serve customers.

Today, corporate web organizations have replaced HTML-based templates with JSP and ASP web "containers." These "extended assets" include complex containers, profiling tools, catalogs and transaction-laden servlets. The demand for the functionality provided by these tools has radically changed the web organization. . . and along with it, the tool-set necessary for deploying and maintaining a healthy web site.

When he discusses the "extended asset," Russell refers to those web objects that the HTML hobbyist or graphic artist can't create. But bringing developers who create these "new assets" into the classical web organization carries some risk, unless consistent, daily integration occurs.

Russell's approach is superior because it is distinctly human. He acknowledges content management as a change process, and identifies each stakeholder's needs before crossing the starting line. After all, each stakeholder has his or her tools of the trade, along with a modus operandi that competes for the attention required by the content management system.

Content managers must make the company's stakeholders want to participate as contributors. My time at Xerox and GE has taught me that unlimited access to a content management system serves as only the starting point. The successful content manager must also provide a "branching structure" that reflects the various contributing roles within the enterprise. Developers, graphic artists, web site producers, external agencies, data modelers, translation professionals, and every other function within the enterprise—particularly sales and product marketing—must all be accounted for.

While the market is experiencing a gut-wrenching reality check, a semblance of normalcy is returning to the web industry and enterprises are taking a sobering look at where their web priorities lie. With a new focus on customers' needs and providing utility to all parts of the product lifecycle, content is rapidly extending beyond the enterprise to both suppliers and customers. The "street" has come to recognize that sales-based web statistics have nothing to do with building a successful, digitized business. Traditional and "new" content—and the mechanisms necessary to make them available to the customer—are ultimately what will determine a company's digital vitality.

Manuel Terranova
Fairfield, CT
August 5, 2001
Manuel_Terranova@yahoo.com

FOREWORD

Russell Nakano is the ideal author for this book. Russell was employee number one at Interwoven. Back in 1996, the two of us shared some pretty ambitious dreams. . . dreams that were borne of the astounding revolution that was taking place at the time, called the World Wide Web. Little did we know that the path to making those dreams a reality would route us through the backs of trailers and the spare corners of friends' hotel rooms, office spaces formerly known as laundromats, and over similarly challenging market terrain, on our way to becoming a $2 billion company.

The need for what we eventually called web content management had become clear to Russell and me long before Interwoven was a familiar name in the web space. As a co-founder of Match.com, I had helped architect, develop, and launch a fairly complex web site. Match.com employed what was then (in the mid-90s) a fairly heady combination of graphics, text, photographs, min-animations, and database content, all supplied by numerous contributors. Prior to Match.com I had built data servers at both Sybase and Illustra.

Through those experiences, and Russell's work writing operating system software for Apple Computer and Taligent, we realized that if a variety of content developers—such as graphic designers, marketing personnel, and software engineers—were trying to put together a web site, there was a huge need to manage the process and the assets. Both of us were software engineers, and we understood the challenges of coordinating large numbers of engineers who had to work on different parts of a software program. But this was a completely different beast than one that could be harnessed by a traditional software configuration management system or a document management system.

The larger web sites had hundreds of people working on hundreds of thousands of files, if not millions of them (a large software system might have ten thousand files). The cycle-time for publishing a new version of a web site was sometimes only hours (as opposed to months for the most aggressive software products). Obviously, there needed to be a formal series of steps for developing, rapidly approving, and deploying content.

Such a "workflow" would guarantee that all content would be published in a timely manner and would protect the content's integrity. . . and, by extension, the integrity of the web site itself. The realization that no existing system for managing collaboration and digital assets could meet the needs of web content management drove us to build Interwoven TeamSite.

Adding a sense of urgency to our endeavors was the web explosion that was taking place at the time. The late '95/early '96 timeframe marked the single most aggressive period of growth in the Internet, and we saw an untapped, potentially enormous market, one that was ramping up at a dizzying speed. Surely, we thought, if all of the companies who were scrambling to deploy sites needed to harness their corporate assets, the sales opportunities for a content management system would be practically limitless. By supporting groups of users with powerful workflows and the efficient development of web content, we felt sure that we had the key to resolving one of the bigger technology challenges of the era.

We began talking with our peers; webmasters in other organizations who were enmeshed in trying to launch their own web sites. When we described the product we were designing, they invariably wanted to buy it. Their responses to our inquiries rapidly convinced us that we'd hit upon a very common (and very strong) need to bring some control to the chaos of building web sites. We continued to keep this need in mind during the formative years of Interwoven. And this ongoing need is the reason why *Web Content Management: A Collaborative Approach* eventually came to be.

I must admit, at the time not everyone shared our vision. In the early days of Interwoven, we made the rounds of what seemed like every venture capitalist on the planet, hoping to fund our budding enterprise. We were convinced that the future of the web would require a radical retooling of existing technologies and quite possibly, the invention of an entirely new one. *Enterprise content management* became the embodiment of this next generation of the web, as we perceived it. But it was extremely difficult to convince people who lacked hands-on involvement in the mission-critical operations of a web site.

If it's any comfort to the start-up visionaries of today, we definitely had our share of tough times in trying to "sell" the vision. We also knew that if any of the bigger software companies decided to develop the same kind of product as ours, we wouldn't have the resources to compete. Luckily, a few brave souls supported our efforts and shared the risks with us. Their courage eventually helped us to define and establish this crucial new category. (It's also earned them a fairly tidy return, I'm happy to say!)

In the ensuing years, Interwoven TeamSite has been built in close partnership, and in countless meetings, with our customers. We've never stopped asking, "What do you need most?" And the answers we receive continue to fuel our innovation. We never set out to create the so-called killer app. Instead, we evolved our technology to meet the unique needs of our customers. Naturally, we did have some general ideas of what needed to be built. But one of the secrets to our success was that we immediately relayed back to development what we heard in the field.

Some of TeamSite's most robust capabilities were, in fact, developed in direct response to discussions with our customers. Over and over again, they've told us that they want to make web content contribution simple, fast, and hassle-free. They want to empower everyone within their organizations, from the most junior marketing staff to the HTML gurus, to create and publish content, so templating proved an ideal solution. They want to ensure that all contributors can check their work, without jeopardizing the work of others. Individual work areas using our smart file system filled the bill. We've never attempted to retrofit existing technology if the solution did not fully meet the needs of our customers. And we have never veered from our original charter to address the content management challenge. From its very inception, TeamSite has mirrored the needs of its users. And these requirements continue to drive the product's evolution.

This book will provide you with the broadest possible perspective on content management. Although TeamSite has become the content management system of choice for hundreds of business leaders around the globe, we recognize that more often than not, the entire category is often still puzzling. Russell and I thought that a book like this one would help demystify the process of deploying and managing enterprise-scale web initiatives. Therefore, I was pleased when I learned that Addison-Wesley also had an interest in having Russell author this book. If customer input is any indication, such clarification is long overdue.

We have come to realize the intrinsic value of sharing the common experiences of all of our customers, prospects, and partners, and our own experiences as web practitioners. So with those goals in mind, Russell has synthesized all of our core thinking and has organized it into an easy-to-use format. Beginning with Interwoven's very first engagements, Russell documented his conversations with our customers, as well as reports from Interwoven's sales team. In these application notes and "use cases," Russell captured customers' biggest concerns, and what was done (from a technology perspective) to resolve them.

These real-life scenarios were referred to, time and time again, by all of Interwoven's product developers, our sales and marketing personnel, and everyone charged with interacting with our customers. We hope this summary of our best practices will provide you with the insights you need to move forward with your own web development.

The past five years at Interwoven have been exhilarating, frustrating, educational, and rewarding. To witness the company's transition from our fledgling days to our position as the market leader in content management seems highly surreal. Our success has been fueled both by the growth of the web market, and the field-proven products we've developed to support it.

But if you ask me what is the most important reason for our success, it would be the people and the culture we built at Interwoven. I am no longer very surprised when new team members come up to me and tell me that Interwoven is the best place in which they've ever worked. Then again, this should not be unexpected if you have been part of a successful web team. A good content management solution is a prerequisite for success, but ultimately it is the people in your team who determine how well you do.

If you're reading this book, you probably have a specific need related to your web presence. You've doubtless already deployed one or more web sites, be they external eBusiness sites, an intranet, extranet, B2B portal, or some other variation thereof. In the process, you've probably discovered the challenge of effectively managing all of the assets that comprise your enterprise's collective corporate knowledge. Without this capability, your web initiatives are typically destined to languish somewhere, unrealized. (Done right, the web becomes a business-critical repository of your corporate knowledge. That is why content infrastructure is now seen as a key component in virtually every company's IT strategy.)

It is to you that we dedicate this book, and we hope that the pages that follow will help your vision become reality. Yours are the needs that we at Interwoven keep in mind, every day. And helping you meet your ongoing web challenge is what our content infrastructure products—especially for content management—are all about.

The World Wide Web is sure to continue its rapid evolution, spawning opportunities for business and personal interactions we can't even conceive of as yet. But what is sure to remain a constant is the requirement to effectively manage your organization's valuable, extensive store of corporate knowledge. We believe that through a collaborative approach—one that supports all users, channels, processes, and initiatives— every enterprise can transform its web content into a strategic corporate asset.

I congratulate Russell on his tremendous dedication and achievement in writing this book. And on behalf of everyone at Interwoven, I wish you success in all of your web initiatives. I trust that this book will smooth your way.

Peng T. Ong
Founder & Chairman
Interwoven, Inc.
July 2001

PREFACE

The Purpose of This Book

This is a book about content management, with an emphasis on web content. More specifically, it's about developing, managing, maintaining and deploying web content solutions across the enterprise. It addresses the questions common to all small, medium, and large enterprises encounter as they grow:

- How can I manage my growing base of web assets?
- How do I get information to my customers, employees, and suppliers quickly?
- How can I ensure that my web site's content is dynamic?
- How can I get all my employees to become active contributors to my web site's success?
- What do I need to do now to ensure my web site is successful?

There have been many books written on managing a web project, understanding web technologies, building a web property, and ensuring usability. Each of them deals with the perplexing challenge of the web by delving deeply into a specific aspect: processes, technology, or people. This book is a combination of all three. It has to be. Content management is a technology solution that's implemented using specific techniques (e.g., workflow analysis, deployment solutions) to ensure wide-scale usability (from web developers to content contributors).

Content makes a web property what it is. This is as true today as it was yesterday. This will continue to be true into the future, even as technological advances create ever more sophisticated ways to run businesses, reach customers, and react to trends. Content defines the soul of the property. Managing content includes the steps to design, create, implement, modify, archive, review, approve, and deploy.

As a founding engineer, system architect, and principal consultant, I have seen content management projects across industries, geographies, and organizations. Most have struggled to manage the tremendous growth in the web space without a corresponding growth in web tools and techniques. Hence the need for a book—a practical guide for project managers and web architects.

This book has taken me two years to write. During that period, I've been involved in over 50 web development projects in various roles with Interwoven, a content infrastructure software company. My involvement ranged from informal e-mail consultation, to in-depth design meetings, to focused implementation efforts, to complete implementation engagements. These experiences exposed me to a wide range of industries and organizations. It became clear that successful content management solutions share common features and are driven by a core set of principles and techniques.

I have attempted to distill my experience and that of my colleagues into this book. It began as a series of application notes that I wrote for Interwoven project managers and technical consultants. The notes explained concepts, principles, and techniques to help guide implementers and managers of web content management solutions. The notes helped our customers and consulting partners to frame and develop their content management solutions. The notes became the backbone of this book. The true test of a book is the number of scribbles in the margins, post-its sticking from various angles, bent corners, along with the occasional coffee spill. I hope this book will receive the same measure of wear-and-tear. If it does, I know that my goal has been accomplished.

Who Should Read this Book

This book will be useful to three broad categories of web practitioners: managers, architects, and developers. Managers benefit from understanding content management for the purpose of structuring the flow of work and planning resource allocation. A development manager needs to know how to separate tasks to minimize interference and how to orchestrate multiple web initiatives. A production manager focuses on streamlining the flow of changes from development, through a review process, to the ultimate destinations on multiple production servers. Accuracy, reliability, and reproducibility are paramount concerns to the production manager. A business manager, especially the executive sponsor of web initiatives, needs to understand how process and infrastructure improvements generate tangible business benefits. Benefits include faster development, more effective use of staff, and greater reliability. All managers benefit from knowing what is possible with current tools.

Architects focus on internal design, integration with other business systems, and technology choices. Throughout the thought process they must pay attention to structuring the design to facilitate rapid development both with the current staff and expanded staff down the road. For these reasons, architects must be cognizant of the precepts of content management. Their goal after all, is to design what can be built, to build what can be assembled quickly, and to assemble what can be tested easily and often.

Developers are specialists who create content as their primary job, such as Java developers or graphic artists, and others who contribute content as an adjunct to their jobs, such as a marketing manager or public relations specialist. A developer who grasps the principles of content management will understand its role in a larger context. This is especially important because a strong developer is inevitably tapped to contribute in the role of lead developer, where understanding the big picture helps to effectively blend the efforts of the group.

The managers, architects and developers who form the primary target of this book collectively have diverse experiences and wide skill sets. This diversity explains the difficulty that sometimes arises in explaining web content management because different people play different roles in the web endeavor. Each category of stakeholder has a different objective, and hence they tend to look at the problem of content management differently. For example, content contributors want the shortest path possible to get their changes to the web, with as few obstacles as possible. In contrast, production managers want to make sure that content is tested, reviewed, and safely under version control. Because of the difference in perspectives, different parts of the content management solution are assigned different priorities. All the views need to be accounted for, striving for a realistic balance.

Organizations are also governed by their current practices. For example, one reader may currently use "edit directly on the production server." A different reader may use the "test changes on a staging server before deploying to production server technique." Others may use the "e-mail content to the webmaster" approach. Part of the challenge is to bring all of these different perspectives up to a common starting point.

Because of all of these differences, finding the initial common ground on which to build the motivation and techniques for content management requires some effort. This includes agreeing on the vocabulary and building a common understanding of the problems. An experienced content management manager or architect will find the early portions of the book a useful refresher on concepts. However, a manager new to content management will find this information invaluable. In addition to setting the stage for later chapters, the book helps frame views on the proper interactions and interrelationships in a true web environment.

One of the important elements of this book is the use of "day-in-the-life-of" examples. New managers will find tremendous value in viewing the practices of other web organizations. These examples are based on companies that I've worked with, and represent a broad cross-section: companies both large and small, from dot-coms to brick-and-mortar companies, from many different industries.

The Art of Content Management

To truly convey the meaning of web content management, we cannot merely talk about tools. This book expands the reader's view to look at people, tools, processes, and organizations as an interrelated whole. That's a big lesson that Interwoven's consulting force has learned over the course of implementing content management for customers over the last three years. It isn't just about installing a tool, loading the content, handing over a stack of manuals, and heading for the exit. Implementing a content management solution is a number of things that are much broader in scope. It is building a partnership between the consultants who understand how to use the product and the customer who understands the social and organizational dynamics of his or her company. It is a fallacy to underestimate the importance of either side of the equation. Building a flawless and pristine installation will not be successful if the implementation effort finds itself blind-sided by an entrenched "not-invented-here" attitude about software tools in general. Similarly, a perfectly aligned organization is useless if there isn't an appreciation of the "art" of managing thousands of web assets, designing effective workflow, and getting that information from content contributors.

That's the challenge and curse of implementing a web content management solution. It is essential to build strong bridges between many constituencies in order to lay a path to success. It can neither be a fully grassroots effort to build a solution from the bottom up without executive sponsorship, nor can it be a top-down solution that is imposed by executive fiat. As with most things in life, there are challenges and struggles in any implementation effort. Without a doubt, the rewards make it worthwhile.

The Science of Content Management

This book primarily speaks to the practice of content management, which differs from the "science" of content management. The term "content management" has only recently been used to refer to the principles and practices around developing, managing, maintaining, and deploying content in an organization. As such, it is more common to find practitioners of content management than scientists of content management. A practitioner slings a toolkit over her shoulder and carries a collection of useful concepts in her head, but her primary objective is to help clients set up an infrastructure to manage content. The practitioner engages with clients, asking questions, sensing the lay of the land, in an attempt to gain insight into which of several approaches to bring to bear on the problem. Success is measured both by how well the implementation matches the original requirements and by how happy the client is. The former tends to be objective, while the latter is hugely subjective. Measuring against requirements moves close to the notion of the science of content management, while client happiness is scientifically unsound.

This dichotomy between the objectively measurable and the scientifically unsound is evident in this book. On one hand, we endeavor to convey the flavor of the practice of content management through experiences gained from numerous client engagements during what will undoubtedly be viewed as the formative years of the Internet revolution. On the other hand, through that limited and possibly idiosyncratic perspective, we strive to distill the common concepts and principles that have proven to be useful across many engagements. Does it rise to the level of science? Probably not. Do I wish that the concept building, hypothesis testing, and strenuous analysis could be infused with enough rigor to qualify as science? Of course. But it is my honest belief that the field isn't quite ready for that degree of consolidation. But just as pioneer farmer might have discerned the science of agriculture, or a village healer might have gleaned the beginnings of the science of medicine, we hope that some of the lessons described here will help others to point the way toward a "science" of content management.

Organization of this Book

This book has ten chapters that divide naturally into three parts. Part One lays out the motivation for content management. It examines the issues that arise when a solution is not in place. It introduces the concepts of content management that will be used throughout the rest of the book. This section paints the essential backdrop for readers unfamiliar with content management concepts. Case study examples highlight the importance of content management in the proper functioning of any organization's web sites. Readers who are more familiar with content management may wish to skim this section to refresh their understanding of the issues, and jump into Part Two for a detailed discussion of theory.

Part Two introduces the concepts and principles required by a practitioner, and provides the framework to develop a content management solution. Technical architects, project managers and consultants will find the basic building blocks for the content management solution within these chapters. This section presents the content management theory necessary to build a solution, used extensively in Part Three. This section starts with the importance of content management in ensuring a collaborative development environment, highlighting the practices that must be encouraged. It follows with a detailed discussion of the key levers of a successful content management solution: templating, workflow, deployment, and branch design. Each of these sections delves into the theory underpinning each content management lever to understand its value within a content management framework, its impact on an organization, and the complexity required to reach a solution. Examples are used to illustrate common uses of each lever within a business context

Part Three explains how to design and implement a content management infrastructure. It describes a step-by-step procedure to generate the implementation architecture, and proposes a task-based methodology to guide the implementation of the agreed-upon design.

Part One—Motivation for Content Management

Chapter One—The Internet Changes the Rules of the Game. Motivates the need for a content management solution.

Chapter Two—Overview of Content Management. An introduction to the concepts of content management used throughout the book. It enables you to understand content management without delving into the details necessary to implement the solution.

Part II—Concepts and Principles

Chapter Three—Principles of Collaborative Web Development. Lays the foundational principles of collaborative development. It covers the core issues of web site versioning, and managing concurrent changes.

Chapter Four—Best Practices for Collaborative Web Development. Describes the work area-staging area-edition paradigm of development, and lays out the four basic work cycles: development, compare/update, review, and test.

Chapter Five—Templating Empowers Content Contributors. Details the rationale for templating, or separation of content from presentation.

Chapter Six—Workflow Speeds Work Cycles. Delves into the benefits and concepts of a workflow infrastructure to speed the development process.

Chapter Seven—Deploying Content. Introduces the concepts that govern a deployment infrastructure. Presents a design for a deployment infrastructure.

Chapter Eight—Multiple Web Initiatives. Covers the concept of branch design, which introduces the notion of a logically independent web site. These concepts address the core issues of project completion skew, and of long-term versus short-term projects. Details how to design a branch structure for multiple web initiatives.

Part Three—Design and Implementation

Chapter Nine—Using Web Content Management for Globalization. Presents design of content management system for a globalization project.

Chapter Ten—Summary and Conclusions. Summarizes what we've learned. Discusses trends in content management and what they imply for the future.

ACKNOWLEDGMENTS

Creating this book took four times longer than originally hoped for and the effort was ten times more strenuous than I would have wished for. But the effort has been worthwhile, in large measure because of the numerous people who have supported this project throughout its lifespan. They all shared the belief that something could be constructed where nothing had existed before.

I owe a debt of gratitude to Peng Ong, who gave me an incredible opportunity to help transform his product vision into software. The initial development team of Kevin Cochrane, Terrence Yee, and Gajanana Hegde steadfastly believed in Peng's vision and provided an intensely creative work environment to launch the product.

Several product releases later, Peng handed me another incredible opportunity: to join his fledgling consulting organization. Robert Gerega, Jennifer Marek, Zhaohong Li, Victoria Chiu, James Koh, Jon Lau, and Robert Turner were extremely supportive of my early efforts to codify knowledge in application notes. I am indebted to our early customers who were willing to put their faith in our people and our products.

I owe thanks to T. Francis Richason, Reza Haniph, Christine Owens, and Raghu Madhok who gave me the time and encouragement to complete the application notes and the manuscript. Marc Carignan deserves mention for being especially supportive and accommodating.

I extend my gratitude to the numerous people who reviewed drafts and provided helpful comments: Adam Stoller, Robert Gerega, Evers Ding, Andrew Chang, Blake Sobiloff, Dave Cadoff, Stan Cheng, Jack Jia, Patrice McCauley, Christine Owens, Dhruv Ratra, Mark Bradley, Raghu Madhok, Kevin Lindbloom, and Anurag Gupta from Interwoven; Mitchel Ahern, Ravishankar Belavadi, Ren Bitonio, Linda Brigman, Jeff Rule, Kenneth Trant Jr., and John Wegis choreographed by Addison-Wesley.

James Koh provided fascinating insights on the birth of a corporate web presence. Wes Modes enthusiastically described his approach to globalization.

This project could not have been completed without the marketing, art direction, artistic, and literary contributions from Ted Fong, Don Wong, Rick Steed, Raina Pickett, Andrew So, Helen Lee, Debbie Ryan, and Marianne Lucchesi. Executive support for this project from Martin Brauns, Marc Carignan, Mike Backlund, Joe Ruck, and Jack Jia was timely and essential.

Executive editor, Mary O'Brien, and her associates Alicia Carey, Curt Johnson, Jacquelyn Doucette, and Chanda Leary-Coutu at Addison-Wesley were tremendous.

Reza Haniph managed the project tirelessly. He deserves extra credit for playing the role of product champion.

Part One

MOTIVATION FOR CONTENT MANAGEMENT

CHAPTER ONE

THE INTERNET CHANGES THE RULES OF THE GAME

I learned there are troubles

Of more than one kind.

Some come from ahead

And some come from behind.

But I've bought a big bat.

I'm all ready, you see.

Now my troubles are going

To have troubles with me.*

—*Dr. Seuss,* I Had Trouble in Getting to
Solla Sollew

Executive Summary

The Internet is changing many of the unwritten rules that businesses have been following, consciously or otherwise. By connecting people and organizations electronically, and by offering new opportunities for businesses to communicate and interact with customers, partners, employees, and even with actual and potential competitors, the Internet forces us all to rethink how we operate and manage web properties. This chapter describes the rules that drive the environment that web development groups live in. The rules compel us to react, and the principles of content management tell us how to react. The principles of content management described in this book are all based on the rules described in Chapter 1.

3

Introduction

Lisa gulps the last of her Monday morning orange juice as her pager buzzes on her kitchen counter. As the web production manager for a computer wholesale distributor, the blinking phone number on the pager display tells Lisa everything she needs to know. This is the third consecutive Monday that she is receiving a page from the morning shift. Same problem again, she thinks to herself, as she reaches for her briefcase and car keys.

Lisa's production group ensures that the corporate web site functions around the clock. Thousands of resellers around the world depend on their web site for maintaining nearly all aspects of the business relationship, including obtaining product information, submitting product orders, and reporting account status.

As she accelerates down the freeway on-ramp, Lisa powers up her cell phone. A brief conversation with the web development manager confirms her suspicions. Sure enough, one of the developers, Mario, has been testing the new section of the web site. When complete, the new area on the corporate home page will allow retail partners to establish promotional links to their own web sites. For the last three weekends, Mario had copied the new code to the internal development web site for testing. In the midst of moving other changes to the live production web site Sunday night, a junior member of Lisa's staff mistakenly moved Mario's changes to production too. Just like that, Mario's changes are visible for anyone visiting the wholesaler's web site to see. As resellers log in, they encounter the inadvertently released section of the site, including broken links, dummy data, and other embarrassing artifacts of Mario's testing.

Lisa has sympathy for the developer, who is, after all, a fresh college graduate. Like the rest of the web development staff, Mario has been instructed to test all changes by copying his changes to the development web site. That procedure works fine for most changes on their web site, such as updating the corporate logo, or fixing the spelling in a reseller announcement. Those kinds of changes take only a few minutes to test, review, and approve. Mario's changes are different because the new files require extensive integration into the rest of the web site. Planning realistically, Mario has estimated it would take several weeks to complete the integration.

"Yes, the vendor partner section of the web site mistakenly went live again today!" Lisa sardonically announces at the Monday morning staff meeting, as she glances around the conference table. "One of my guys is removing it from the production servers as we speak—New York, London, Los Angeles, and Hong Kong," she mumbles with embarrassment.

Overview

Behind every web property, behind every business initiative on the web, there are resourceful people working hard to make a web site look good, function well, and most importantly, fulfill a business goal. This book focuses on these people and the tools and processes that they use. These individuals have widely divergent skill sets; they must coordinate across departments, endure extreme time pressure, toil on high-visibility projects, and collaborate across time zones and geography. Yet they work tirelessly to harness the opportunity offered by the Internet age. They are the production crew behind the scenes. They are the heroes of our story.

The Internet age owes itself to the confluence of technological and social forces that drive communication and interaction between organizations and people from around the globe. As the modern-day "killer application," the web browser takes its place alongside the newspaper, radio, telephone, and television as a fundamental conduit for communication. The vast number of online destinations outstrips the ability of any one person to view them all, which forces web operators to compete fiercely for each person's capricious attention: his or her "eyeballs." The Internet's universal connectivity amplifies the power of the browser, supplying the vast number of eyeballs that power the creation of the myriad of web properties to which we've become accustomed. More properties attract more eyeballs, which justifies greater investment in network connectivity, and further justifies the creation of diverse web properties. This cycle reinforces itself. Greater investment attracts more eyeballs, which justifies more investment. This is an example of the "network effect."[1] It is not a fad.

Hardly anything about web properties stays the same. Once upon a time brochure-ware ruled the day. Then personalization and dynamic web sites supplanted so-called static web sites. Inevitably, this too will be replaced by a different, better technological solution. When online stores emerged on the Internet landscape, it was a novelty to place an order via the Internet. Customers gained the advantage of accessing product information online, bypassing the delay of mailing a catalog order form. But with more entrants in the increasingly crowded arena, consumers have come to expect more: online product availability status, improved search and comparison, order status tracking, and so forth. The future promises continued innovation. Entire companies have rebranded themselves as "e-companies" to gain customer mindshare in the Internet space.[2]

Behind the scenes, web server software has matured. Static HTML and CGI-based sites have been gradually replaced with application servers from vendors that didn't even exist a few years ago. Application servers have gained increasing acceptance

---

[1] Paul Kedrosky, "The network effect," *The Industry Standard*, July 23, 1999.

[2] Rational Software's tag line is "the E-development Company." Informix Inc.'s tag line is "the way to web."

because they offer improved ability to build personalized web sites, increase scalability, and program the "business logic" that drives a modern web site. Server hardware has improved. Operating systems have evolved. Teams are larger, and skills have become more specialized. Departments have expanded, and operations have spread over the country and around the world. Web initiatives have expanded in scope, while implementation schedules have shortened.

Inside each web property lies the world of web development. It is difficult work, involving many contributors working under pressure, with short deadlines. In large measure, web development groups face difficulties because conventional rules no longer apply. They operate under a new set of rules, imposed on them from their environment. A group attempting to follow rules and behaviors that worked in the past inevitably stumbles. The purpose of this book is to explain the rules and to help avoid the stumbles.

Fear and Greed

In late 1999, a web producer at a web development agency attends a meeting with the executive of a large retail establishment. The purpose of the meeting is to discuss ways that the web agency's development team could build a web presence for the retail operation. Does the executive believe in the Internet? Not really, the executive admits. He consents to exploratory discussions regarding an Internet presence because of the fear that one of his competitors will outmaneuver him in the Internet space.

It is an old saying that two fundamental forces move the financial markets: fear and greed. These same irresistible forces of human nature drive activities in the Internet space. The executive just described acts because of fear that a competitor will reach his customer base before his organization has time to effectively respond. Others like him drive forward ambitiously because of greed, to commandeer a "first-mover"[3] market presence in a hot segment of a business before multiple participants settle into the hand-to-hand combat of daily business operations.

The anecdote about the executive illustrates the irresistible force that the web exerts on a modern business to change. One measure of the strength of a force is its ability to move an unwilling participant. By this measure the executive found himself moved by fear. Many other organizations have been similarly influenced. We cannot say for

---

[3] M. Lieberman and D. Montgomery, "First-mover advantages," *Strategic Management Journal*, 9, pp. 41–58, 1988. Jeff Moore, "The book on first-mover advantage," http://www.clickz.com/cgi-bin/qt.article.html?article=871, October 26, 1999. For opposing views, see James Fallows, "The first mover myth," *The Industry Standard*, September 17, 1999, and David Simons, "The mythology of first-mover advantage," January 3, 2000.

certain that the retail executive enjoyed success in his half-hearted endeavor. Perhaps his effort eventually fizzled. But the dynamics driving an industry require only that one participant in a given industry, through genius or sheer luck, assemble the team, the resources, and the business opportunity to capitalize on the possibilities presented by the Internet. Their success sets the standard for other participants to follow. It doesn't matter whether the standard-bearer is a newcomer to the industry or a long-time industry stalwart, the first pioneer to establish a successful beachhead sets the standard for the rest.

Rules of the Game

To be successful, web development groups need to learn the rules required for surviving and thriving in the new environment. Each rule illustrates an essential reality in the transformation of business processes as companies incorporate the Internet into everyday work. Because these rules govern the basic precepts of the Internet, familiarity with these rules will be essential to an understanding of the discipline of content management.

Rule #1: It's the Assets, Stupid!

Founded in 1927, W.W. Grainger is one of the largest business-to-business (B2B) players. It sells 220,000 maintenance, repair, and operating (MRO) items through 500 stores to 1.5 million customers. Its annual sales run at $4.7 billion. Back in 1995 the Grainger management team seeded the web operation with an initial infusion of $5 million. Today 150 people work in the online operation, and in 2000 it expected to do $200 million in business over the web.[4]

The key to Grainger's e-commerce franchise goes far beyond digitizing the content contained in its red phonebook-sized paper catalog that lets businesses browse and order items ranging from axes, to rubber boots, to voltmeters. Digitized catalog items, consisting of images, textual descriptions, and pricing information, are the most highly visible asset. But the value goes much deeper. The Grainger site hosts information areas that range from hurricane preparedness tips to proper care of power tools. These help areas put a friendly face on the staid corporate look, and they build traffic and goodwill with customers. Behind the item information lies item availability information, search keys, and indexing information that power the search and indexing capability, which is a key differentiation for the online catalog, as compared with the traditional paper catalog. Finally, application code drives the entire web experience; it defines the business logic that governs ordering, shipping, and cus-

---

[4] Douglas Blackmon, "Selling motors to mops, unglamorous Grainger is a web-sales star," *The Wall Street Journal*, December 13, 1999, p. B1.

tomer account management. Running a web operation of the magnitude of the Grainger site requires a wide range of assets, many of which aren't directly visible but nonetheless are indispensable components of the operation.

It is the web site assets, taken together, that form the assets of the Grainger web property. They are irreplaceable. The business cannot function without them. At the same time, the assets change. Some assets change frequently. For example, a hurricane preparedness site and a blizzard preparedness site are seasonal. Some assets change less frequently. For example, a new corporate privacy policy introduces new logic to the ordering sequence, and that logic remains intact for years. Above all, the constant evolution captures the collective learning of the entire organization. The web assets embody this learning. The web and associated server give the assets life, which in turn express the organization's collected wisdom in an active form.

Rule #2: Experiment. Iterate. Grow.

A corporate research and development center is an unlikely location for cutting-edge forays into novel business models, but that's exactly where innovation began in a multi-billion dollar global transportation and logistics company in 1994. A researcher inadvertently steered two very different worlds onto a collision course. One of those worlds was the public Internet, the outpost of freewheeling renegades operating at lightning speed at the boundaries of the law, or sometimes beyond. The other world was the corporate back-office, a place traditionally dominated by big-iron mainframe computers and buttoned-down security procedures. After uniting the two worlds, vast possibilities unfolded that companies routinely exploit today.

So what was the historic act? The researcher rigged a web server outside the corporate firewall to query package shipment status and to present the result on a web page. Armed with a shipper's package identifier number, a sender and recipient can instantly determine the exact whereabouts of their package along its journey from sender to recipient. It was a revolutionary idea. If a Hollywood screenwriter had scripted the event, the protagonist would have grasped thick cables in each hand and brought them together in an explosion of sparks.

A quiet revolution followed when the researcher built an integrated system to present detailed information about package shipment status hosted on a corporate mainframe. Connecting the corporate back-office to a newfangled web server attached to the public Internet opened the door to countless innovations to follow.

From the moment that the two worlds fused, the ensuing events moved in a way that has been repeated in many businesses and organizations, in many different forms. A new force emerges, which compels organizations to embrace the Internet as a medium for disseminating information, realizing commerce opportunities, and bringing new opportunities to fruition. Just as innovations of the past, such as steel making, the railroad, or the telephone, opened the doors for new arrangements of people and resources and new business opportunities, the Internet causes gradual yet unmistakable realignment of operations.

Here is the irony: The researcher was merely goofing around. It is unlikely that he fully grasped the immense repercussions of his actions. Instead, he modestly set about to demonstrate the feasibility of public access to up-to-the-minute internal logistics data over the Internet. The technology allowed it. The opportunity was there. He seized it.[5]

Several years later the business model pioneered by the transportation and logistics company would be given a name: *online customer self-service*. In this model, customers use the Internet to access a web property that allows them to track the status of an in-transit package whenever they choose. The corporation reaps benefits because the new service is a low-cost and efficient way to improve the responsiveness of its customer service operation.

This example is instructive. The researcher's actions brought dramatic changes. This example illustrates an important lesson that it is vital for web development teams to remember. Big changes sometimes begin with goofing around. An artist experiments with a new juxtaposition of graphic elements. A developer tries out a different twist on a Flash-enabled page. A SQL developer wants to try a different variation about presenting the results from a query. Big changes arise from small innovations. Each contributor needs a place to try out these changes without needing to endanger the entire organization's effort by having everyone share a common staging server.

Iterative development, proven to be immensely valuable to developers, is even more valuable to web developers. Innovation springs from experimentation and iteration. That is a fundamental truth of web development.

Rule #3: Respond to Customers Quickly and Frequently, or Lose Them!

Move ahead to 1996. Inspired by the early work of the playful researcher, the global transportation and logistics company builds package tracking into their public web site. The distinctive feature gains popularity among the customer base. The company touts the ability to track packages as a unique service offering. The package-tracking site has become part of the company's public persona.

Meanwhile, the success of the web site brews another problem. The staff to support the web site has expanded to include more than a dozen people in three departments. Marketing scopes the requirements for the site, and engages with outside vendors to implement its look-and-feel. Information technology incorporates changes,

---

[5] James Koh, personal communication, August 10, 2000.

integrates with the mainframe connectivity code, and takes responsibility for the day-to-day management of the web assets. The operations group moves the modified assets onto the multiple production servers, and they maintain 24×7 uptime.

Changes pour into the site to respond to customer feedback and new marketing requirements. Uptime must be maintained throughout. Efforts of dozens of contributors from three different organizations must be coordinated. Incidents that require immediate attention by the operations staff occur more frequently. Handling emergency fixes to the external web site becomes a daily routine. Everyone realizes that there needs to be a better way.

This is a recurring theme of web development. Early experimentation yields promising results, which encourage larger and more formal business initiatives. Initial efforts are usually modest, involving small staffs and humble resource expenditure. Follow-on efforts involve more people and bigger budgets. Time pressures swell. The stakes escalate. The coordination difficulty magnifies, and the cost of failure is greater. Management pays more attention, compounding the level of stress felt by everyone.

Operators in the Internet space push the envelope of what has been done before, beyond commonly standard practice. The pace of change is relentless. The practice of content management embraces the need for rapid turnaround because inferior efforts are discovered and punished, often in real-time. The Internet encourages side-by-side comparisons of web properties.

Let's see how this works in a simple example. Suppose you have an inkjet printer, and you need to purchase a replacement ink cartridge. You decide to purchase over the Internet. You have many online vendors to choose from. Let's suppose that you haven't settled on a vendor that you have come to rely on for price, delivery, and ease of online ordering. You probably do what many others have done, which is to simultaneously browse multiple online stores. You type the brand of your printer. You probably don't know the manufacturer's part number. You obviously don't know which vendor will have your item in stock.

You decide to shop two sites side by side. Shop one site in one window, and while you wait, you open a second window to visit a second site. Side by side online shopping is unlike shopping in the brick-and-mortar world. Store operators in the physical world understand clearly that each step that you take into their store increases the likelihood that you'll complete your purchase there. If you ask a clerk for assistance and your request is ignored, you might make a quick getaway to a competing store.

In the online scenario, if the search mechanism on one site is clunky, your attention drifts to the other site. If the application server behind one site is slow to render the page, if the servers are overloaded, or if the flavor of JavaScript used on the page isn't compatible with your browser, you'll be favoring the other site in no time at all. If both sites display the correct ink cartridge, but one site cannot tell you whether the item is in stock, the likelihood of completing your order with that vendor drops significantly. If one web site cannot tell you how many days before you'll receive your shipment in the mail, or if the unit price looks good but the shipping cost totals out to a higher final cost, your business evaporates. A recent study by Andersen Consulting suggests that nearly 90 percent of online shoppers had abandoned a shopping basket at least once during a shopping season.[6] Another survey by Boston Consulting Group and Shop.org reveals that 65 percent of online shoppers abandon their filled shopping basket without purchasing.[7]

Not every consumer engages in side-by-side shopping. But its availability points up the fact that web properties must always be vigilant to rapid defection of their customer base. Savvy web operators avoid this defection by rapidly updating their sites' functionality. What was not fully comprehended yesterday becomes plainly obvious when customer feedback pours in, direct or otherwise. This type of rapid feedback has serious implications for the already overloaded web development staff. The staff is delayed by requests for changes. Changes that can be completed quickly must be completed quickly. Changes must be tested, reviewed, approved, and moved into production. This must be done correctly, precisely, and with carefully orchestrated actions. Wasted motion must be avoided. Efficiency is everything.

Rule #4: Enable the Masses!

In 1996, the South of Market Area of San Francisco gestates a significant new web property. It is the home of a groundbreaking web publication, which produces online content that combines the talents of writers, artists, editors, and developers to create a web-based virtual magazine. Unlike traditional publishing, the Internet and web technologies distribute content instantaneously to readership around the world. In this case too, experimentation is rampant. Different graphic layouts, different navigation schemes, different approaches to integrating search, and different editorial styles are all used. For example, the three-area page layout style commonly employed today evolved during that era of experimentation and consisted of a header, a left-side navigation area, surrounding a main content area.[8]

In the next stage, traffic to the property booms. Scores of talented contributors occupy an upper floor of a renovated brick factory building. Computers, monitors, tables, and office chairs cram into a bustling open-air working space. Editors, artists, and developers assemble edgy pieces for an avant-garde readership. Building repeat traffic to the site requires content that changes frequently and involves breaking away

---

[6] Stephanie Izarek, "Fire up your shopping cart," *Computer Shopper*, April 13, 2000.

[7] Jennifer Rewick, "E-tailers try to keep shoppers from bolting at checkout point," *wsj.com*, October 9, 2000.

[8] "Web interface design—The early days of HotWired," WebChicago 2000 Conference & Exposition, March 30, 2000.

from the long editorial cycles familiar to magazine publishing. Content-wise it is a magazine, but its publication cycle makes it unlike anything that preceded it. Virtual "issues" are published daily, sometimes hourly.

The contributors gleefully embrace the rapid pace of change. But the breakneck publication cycle slowly spins out of control. Work is overwritten. Changes are lost. Mistakes once corrected reappear.

A Draconian mandate establishes a stopgap solution. A production manager decrees that there shall be seven prescribed folders on a designated file server. Each folder shall contain work products at a particular point in the development process. When work is complete at one stage, the intermediate work products are to be dragged to the folder representing the next stage. Nominally, a project takes seven days to move through all the stages. From the folder representing the final stage, the content goes to a staging server, where final quality assurance and approval takes place. If approved, the content is copied into production on multiple redundant web servers. In the ideal scenario, each project moves methodically from folder to folder, projects don't depend on each other, and projects don't move backwards. Frustration sets in when the editorial realities intrude and files need to be handled out-of-sequence.

Soon it's obvious that there's a need for a better way to handle concurrent development by scores of contributors, although the folder solution still represents the most basic strategy. The creatives gravitate toward the Macintosh, whose operating system popularized the paradigm of dragging files between folders. The developers edit text files directly on Unix workstations. The seven-folder solution is merely a stopgap until a better solution can be devised. Anything is better than allowing uncontrolled change.

This is another recurring theme of web development. The simultaneous contributions from scores of developers must be managed in a fast-paced environment.

Rule #5: Make It Manageable and Reproducible

Barron looks at his watch. It is going to be tight. Although it is late at night on the East Coast, in just a few hours it will be morning at the London offices, and employees will click open the daily online company newsletter to read the breaking story about the restructuring. But it isn't the news story that worries Barron.

He has survived many restructurings in his career. In fact, Barron takes comfort in realizing that his business unit's express charter is to make sure that business-critical web content shows up correctly, at the right time, with enough bandwidth to supply the demand. His unit has put together a pretty efficient operation, he reflects proudly.

The CEO recorded a company-wide announcement earlier that evening in their corporate headquarters in Manhattan. The address has gone longer than was originally planned, which is the source of Barron's concern. Because of the longer duration, and because of the accompanying web assets to be placed on the Intranet web servers, the network performance experts expect a higher-than-expected load on the multiple streaming video servers placed around the globe. Standard procedure is to use an automated content deployment system to pre-position media files on servers strategically placed at key locations in the firm's global network. In order to handle the higher load without choking the entire network, Barron's group has been summoned to assist.

It is only because of the deployment infrastructure that Barron's group has built that they can respond by deploying the CEO's address and the associated web assets on additional servers. Barron can hardly believe that all of this has taken place the same day. All morning information technology staffers at key locations around the world bring new content server machines online. By the time testing of the new capacity is completed, only a few hours remain to specify the additional machines to receive the deployment.

Barron is proud of the decentralized administration. A crew in each geographic region has the ability to add the new machines to the local deployment tables. When each group finishes, they indicate their readiness. The first call comes in from the Hong Kong office. Barron isn't surprised; it is the middle of their workday. When the final call comes from the London crew, they are ready to proceed.

Barron wants to verify that the new capacity has been brought online.

"Let's edit the homepage for the corporate online newsletter," he suggests to Sarah. Sarah is the lead designer for the online newsletter. Her eyes scan the page for something innocuous to change. Her eyes stop at the text "Jan 10," which she deftly edits to "10-Jan".

"Let's push this change out now." Sarah suggests. Barron agrees. Both of them know what will happen next. Because Sarah designated this change a high-priority change, the modified homepage is immediately copied to Intranet servers around the world. Within a minute, Sarah's pager beeps. The message confirms that the modified page has been successfully deployed to all servers, including the new ones that have been brought online that evening.

They are nearly done. The servers are operational, and the content has been fully approved before the close of the business that day.

continued

Sarah directs the content management system to schedule a deployment of the CEO's video announcement to the Intranet web servers to coincide with 7 A.M. London time. She double-checks that her pager will be notified if any problems were to occur. Since the corporate communications group wants the announcement to be released no earlier than 7 A.M., but no later than 8 A.M., that will give an extra hour if something goes wrong.

"Are you going to hang around to watch the deployment?" Sarah asks Barron.

"Won't be necessary," he replies. "How about if we grab some dinner? You'll be automatically paged if anything goes wrong along with the other content administrators in Hong Kong, London, and New York!"

It seems contradictory. web processes use new formulas. Experimentation and spontaneity are necessary ingredients in the mixture. Providing the opportunity for new recipes to catch on implies that there is a freedom to experiment, to try new things. But at the same time, an ongoing business needs to preserve fully functioning operations even as hotbeds of innovation within an organization try out new ways to capitalize on web opportunities.

On the surface it sounds paradoxical, but studies of human group performance indicate that people need a combination of freedom and structure to achieve at their highest level.[9] Analyses of high-achieving corporate cultures suggest that balance is key. A culture that is too freewheeling tends to falter because of lack of coordination. It neglects the basic tasks that make an organization work. Because there are no established procedures for most things, some groups excel, while others get into trouble.

At the other extreme, a culture that requires controls and procedures for everything becomes too process bound, and the result is uninspired performance. Studies suggest that process and structure are beneficial, up to a point. It's best to introduce enough process to ensure that the efforts of individuals and groups coordinate with minimal wasted effort, but refrain from adding process where it hinders more than it helps, or if it prevents the spark of insight from igniting a better way to do things.

This same principle applies to web operations. The ideal is to encourage enough disruptive chaos to allow your organization to capitalize on chance connections, but introduce an infrastructure that builds web assets in a manageable and reproducible manner.

The requirement for manageability and reproducibility sits alongside the imperatives outlined earlier, which compounds the difficulty. If we follow the other rules, but neglect this one, we have an incomplete recipe. If we fail to build an infrastructure that manages the fast-paced, innovative, and diverse environment that we've put

---

[9] Gary Hamel, *Leading the Revolution*, Harvard Business School Press, Boston, Massachusetts, 2000.

together, we'll find that groups trip over one another, and productivity suffers. Moreover, in the hyper-speed, talent-scarce world of web development, building a manageable and reproducible practice fosters a happy, productive workforce.

Summary

Let's summarize the rules that successful web operators must follow:

1. It's the assets, stupid!
2. Experiment. Iterate. Grow.
3. Respond to customers quickly and frequently, or lose them!
4. Enable the masses!
5. Make it manageable and reproducible.

The rules reflect the changing nature of web properties. First, web assets of your organization distill the content and logic of the operation. The web unifies previously separate efforts. In a commerce web property, marketing and product information previously were the province of the marketing group. For example, marketing produces assets, such as price lists and brochures. Separately, the information technology group maintains equally important supply-chain and order-management systems, such as application programs and database update scripts that run those systems. With the Internet, these previously separate efforts are united within a web-based operation.

Second, the Internet forces assets to evolve rapidly and keep up with the mercurial environment. Visitors to a web property have come to expect rapid change. They expect fresh content and frequently upgraded service offerings, as well as new, more powerful functionality. Because they expect it to be so, operators of web properties are compelled to fulfill those expectations.

Third, try different approaches through experimentation and iteration at all levels. Because of the newness of the technologies and the novel possibilities that they introduce, there isn't an unequivocal right and wrong way of doing things. Your customers always want more. At the microscopic level, individual contributors try different layouts and navigational models to see how they look and feel. At the macroscopic level, web teams introduce new features and then tweak them based on actual usage.

Fourth, the web brings together a diverse band of contributors. The talents of writers, developers, artists, and marketers combine to infuse life into a modern web property. People contribute in many roles and capacities: as full-time employees, as contractors, as outside vendors, and as independent "stringers."

Fifth, the content management infrastructure binds the mixture together as the "glue" that makes the process manageable and reproducible. Just as Fredrick Taylor espoused the "scientific management" of manufacturing enterprises in the early

1900s,[10] web content management is likewise a principled approach to management of a web property.

As we will see in the coming chapters, the process of developing and managing a web property can be codified into a collection of best practices.

Roadmap

Here is a roadmap for the remaining chapters. Chapter 2 gives an overview of content management, and how its practices boost efficiency of an organization. Chapter 3 illustrates how web development organizations of different sizes face different problems related to content management. Chapter 4 explains the basic principles of content management. Chapter 5 explains the benefits of a templating subsystem. Chapter 6 shows the benefits of a workflow subsystem, and how to approach the high-level design of a workflow specification. Chapter 7 explains the benefits of a deployment subsystem, and shows how to approach the high-level design. Chapter 8 explains how to support multiple web initiatives through an appropriate branch structure. Chapter 9 provides design example for a globalization initiative. Chapter 10 summarizes the concepts.

---

[10] Fredrick Winslow Taylor, *The Principles of Scientific Management*, Dover Publications, Mineola, New York, 1998, originally published by Harper & Brothers, New York and London, 1911.

CHAPTER TWO

OVERVIEW OF CONTENT MANAGEMENT

It's been a hard day's night,

And I've been working like a dog. *   *—John Lennon and Paul McCartney*

Beyond the mountains

there are again mountains.   *—Haitian proverb*

Executive Summary

The best way to understand content management is to watch a web team in action. This chapter tells a story about a team that manages a web property; it shows how the assets evolve over several years from an exploratory prototyping effort into an enterprise-critical business operation. As the story unfolds, we highlight the core issues of content management via commentary to illustrate how each issue originates, and to point out the approach the team takes to overcome the challenge.

17

From Prototype to Enterprise

It has been a wild four years. Rita's original idea was to build a web site in her spare time to improve the wooden suggestion box outside her company's lunchroom. Over the years, the penciled suggestions on scraps of paper yielded insightful ways to improve product quality, manufacturing efficiency, and employee morale, to name a few. The suggestions bypassed the traditional chain of command, and although the suggestions were almost always anonymous, Rita's group tirelessly made special efforts to respond seriously to each one. Perhaps the reason the aging wooden receptacle led to the changes that it did was the immediacy of the follow-up. Paradoxically, her group had never been formally charged with being the keepers of the suggestion box. It just seemed to be the right thing to do. Rita herself could not have predicted the events that would follow.

2 A.M. Software

It is 1996, and the Internet Age has dawned. No one in the company recalls where the idea came from, but perhaps it doesn't matter. Why not augment the wooden suggestion box with a web site? That way, employees outside that immediate location can participate as well. Rita takes on the challenge during evenings and weekends. She refers to it as "2 A.M. software."

As a skunkworks project, word of the web site's existence spreads by word of mouth and internal e-mail. The suggestion box web site enjoys a steadily increasing flow of visitors. At first, visitors from other company locations visit to see first-hand how the democracy of ideas within that humble support facility can lead to tangible improvements. Soon thereafter, suggestions from other sites begin trickling in. Many of the suggestions pertain to company-wide operations.

Rita is the sole part-time web developer on the project. Just prior to leaving for an out-of-town conference, she demonstrates a prototype to a group of product managers to explain the value of the suggestion system. The product managers offer many suggestions to improve the usability of the interface. After returning from the out-of-town conference, Rita dives into implementing their recommendations.

Without the usual distracting chatter of phone conversations filling the air, Rita adds the pull-down menus to the entry page surprisingly easily. She likes the way that her new menus remove the visual clutter from the page. Eager to show off the new interface, she asks a colleague to try it out. When he tries it, Rita realizes that she hadn't tested her changes with the Netscape browser. They notice that her menus don't erase properly. Because she hasn't tested regularly with different browsers, some new code she recently added is the likely culprit. But which change is it?

The one-week hiatus renders Rita's recollection about the web site internals hazy. She needs help recalling what worked and what didn't work when she last did the demo. Luckily, Rita versioned the entire source tree of the demo web site before leaving on her trip. She's able to figure out what changes are candidates for the browser sensitivity that seems to have been induced by her recent changes.

Web site versioning plays a crucial role in the web development process. It is essential to periodically capture known snapshots of the web site, as we see in Rita's early efforts with the web site. Snapshots serve several purposes. First, with a known snapshot of the web site a developer can roll back to a known-good copy of the web site. Second, if the web site or a section of it becomes hopelessly broken, a developer needs to be able to selectively pick assets to revert to. An *asset* is an electronic artifact that embodies the intellectual property of an organization. Having a known working set of web assets lets a developer proceed to make changes with the assurance that there's always the ability to compare to a working copy for ongoing development. A working copy can be used as a reference copy, to discern what changed and what didn't. Typically, only a small fraction of a set of files changes from one day or week to the next, which makes having a reference working copy of a web site invaluable for locating the changes that led to a problem. The core issue of site versioning typically arises distinctly early in a web site's lifecycle.

The Pioneers

The team expands to four members. Rita is now the web architect, an informal leader of her band of renegades. They soon find themselves doing independent tasks. Sandy is the quality assurance leader whose primary goal is to build a test harness for the business logic embedded in the web application. She has also volunteered to prototype the online help system. Max is the CGI developer, and he is converting the text-file-based suggestion repository to use the corporate-standard commercial database. James is the interface designer, and he explores ways to simplify the interface.

continued

It is Tuesday. James breezes past the unattended reception desk. He hears a few clattering keyboards from the early risers in the office. As he settles into his cubicle, he listens to the reassuring sound of the coffee maker gurgling the morning's first pot of coffee. James reloads the page that he changed yesterday before he went home.

"What happened to my changes?" James cries out, as he throws his hands into the air. He rechecks the URL to verify that he's indeed pointing at the right location. The reality sinks in. Someone has overwritten his changes with their own changes last night. James gets to his feet. He silently paces the aisle.

Later that day, after much wrangling, the team decides to adopt a practice that gives each developer separate areas to do their work. James does his best to recreate his changes from memory.

Two months pass. The team works 18 hours per day 7 days per week to prepare for their presentation to a corporate Internet task force. To build the team's pitch, Rita gathers recent examples of business improvements that gathered momentum from their web site. She hopes to solicit support from the high-level executives charged with selecting and funding a promising set of web initiatives identified by the Internet task force.

James has numerous changes to the homepage file, `index.html`, and to the first-level pages, such as `suggest.html`, to deliver the promise of his slick new user interface. Max has changes, too. Although he has been working independently and in relative isolation on his database subsystem, it is now time to integrate that code into the homepage and first-level pages as well.

They hammer out an integration plan on Friday after their weekly status meeting, but when 2 A.M. Sunday morning comes around, Max finds that James hasn't completed the changes that they agreed to. James has either forgotten, or his progress was delayed. Unfortunately, when Max snoops around in the directories on James' development machine, he sees various versions of half-completed sets of pages. Max is stuck. He has to either make guesses about what James intended to do, or he needs to call James at home. He relishes neither option. He had intended to finish his integration Saturday night because he promised to help with his niece's sleepover birthday party on Sunday.

We see the issue of *managing concurrent changes* coming to the fore when the group reaches four members. Because each person is off doing different projects, and especially because of the nature of web technologies, they hit a "web-wall." This is the point in the lifecycle of a web site when the combination of the number of developers, the number of assets, and the pace of development exceeds the ability of informal coordination mechanisms to adequately do the job.

The Tornado

Named a finalist by the Internet task force, the team gains additional funding, and grows to 20. The pace of change outstrips the ability of any single person to keep track of changes. As of August 1998 the team is tackling the following projects:

1. Converting to template UI for rebranding
2. Writing scripts to regenerate the UI
3. Implementing better help system
4. Reimplementing form entry based on templates
5. Building client portal

Each project involves a cross-functional team of two to four developers. The project to regenerate the template-based user interface has a scripting component, an HTML component, and a user interface design aspect. Keeping track of any one of these projects on its own would be difficult enough, but keeping track of any two of these projects simultaneously is beyond the grasp of a single person. All five projects taken together require major infrastructure assistance.

In August, James leads a three-person project to convert to a template-based user interface for branding purposes. The release date is near, and the team is deeply involved in testing. Meanwhile, Joe leads a two-person team getting started on implementing the help system. The help team feels strongly about checking in partial releases of their subsystem. Because they have the suggestion system itself to receive client feedback on their help system, they feel that the potential gains outweigh the risks. The help team has content that has been approved and is ready to send to production. On the day before that, the template team plans to have their subsystem ready.

Project completion skew occurs as the team grows to a point that individuals are doing different things and multiple groups each have a different project focus. In other words, each project is coping with contributors on a project who are working on diverse activities, and each project alone has a need to develop, integrate, test, and review their work before their project can be integrated into the live web site. Inevitably, projects run concurrently, and they don't all finish at the same time. One project might be getting underway while another project prepares to wrap up their work. There needs to be a way to keep the work separate.

This problem became especially acute for Rita's group when James and Joe led separate projects. The changes from one project interfered with the other. Because they hadn't introduced separate edit areas, some of the unfinished changes for the branding project mixed in with the finished changes for the new help system. The mixture of finished and unfinished work proved problematic.

> Joe works with the marketing department to build a weekly news section of the web site. For the first few weeks, Joe moves the weekly updates to the production site himself every Saturday at midnight. When that becomes tiresome, he and James agree to share duties on alternate weeks. It gets worse when the marketing department decided to push changes more frequently, now three times per week: a Monday edition, a mid-week edition, and a weekend edition of the newsletter. Both of them agree that they need a more automated system. One day over lunch, they wish for a system that will deploy precisely the assets that they specify, at a predetermined time, and to notify them by pager if the automated system encounters errors.

Deployment comprises the processes and practices by which web assets that have been reviewed and approved are copied from a development environment to a production environment. The goal of a deployment infrastructure is to copy assets to the production server into the right location at the appropriate time. Assets no longer on the development side are deleted from the production side.

An important organizational underpinning of a deployment infrastructure is the "release agreement," which binds the development and production groups into a social contract.[1] Content and application developers agree to approve and formally submit any asset to be deployed, and production server administrators agree to use only released assets on a production server. In a well-designed deployment infrastructure, only someone that is authorized to initiate a deployment job does so. A well-designed deployment infrastructure copies assets into production with minimal or no effort, with full control, notification, and the ability to roll back to a known-good version.

Rita's gang needs an efficient and reliable deployment mechanism almost from the very beginning. Although moving a handful of files to production is simple when taken in isolation, the small overworked staff soon finds itself buried in small trivial tasks that nonetheless are prone to error. It becomes especially difficult when the person copying the files isn't the one who made the changes and therefore isn't familiar with the files.

---

[1] Chapter 7 discusses the release agreement in more detail.

With multiple editions of the newsletter per week, and the increased visitor volume, a misstep in the handling of the numerous content sources is bound to happen. Sure enough, it happens at a particularly inopportune time. The company brass had quietly begun investigating the feasibility of selling the web operation to outside buyers, or alternatively, conducting a public offering. Therefore, it is especially embarrassing that the lead article on a Monday edition of the newsletter misspells the company name of a new partner company. Worse still, it incorrectly identifies the job titles of three of that company's executives.

Workflow is the process by which people collaborate to develop assets within a content management system.[2] This issue becomes important when several people collaborate on a job, where wait time is a significant proportion of the total job time, and where patterns of interaction are repeated frequently. Workflow improves productivity by minimizing the wait time between successive steps, and it automates the business logic of an organization.

One important benefit of workflow is its ability to automate routing, review, and approval of jobs. A second benefit is the ability to enforce a formal business process, as the web operation becomes larger. This advantage becomes especially important when the operation spans different departments.

Rita's group introduces a formal workflow system after the misspelling fiasco in the online newsletter feature article. The rapid growth in the staff justifies investing in a workflow solution because it ensures that each set of changes has had proper review and approval.

Go Dot-com

Rita's department spins out as an independent corporation in April, 1999. The marketers adopt a dot-com name, ezSuggestionBox.com. Previously, they were a division of a small manufacturing company building educational aids for K–12 and the higher education markets. Now they are an independent 100-plus person company. Their customer base is growing, and they have seven major initiatives moving at web-speed simultaneously. The industry analysts refer to them as an "application service provider" in the untapped higher-education market segment. Inside the company, they realize that their growth and ultimate survival as a standalone company rest on their ability to continually enhance and extend their service offering, while maintaining their 24 × 7 uptime promise.

continued

---

[2] Chapter 6 discusses workflow in more detail.

Some of the company's initiatives immediately change the current web site. For example, without advance notice, the marketing group decides to insert a series of banners on the homepage calling attention to an improved notification service. Other initiatives move at a more deliberate pace, such as the ongoing effort to completely replace the homegrown script-based notification system with a commercial product from a third-party vendor.

Each banner project goes from conception, to assignment, to implementation, to review, and to approval within four hours, through the rollout of the new service. But the integration of the commercial notification engine takes six weeks. Neither change can afford to wait for the other.

The issue of *long-term versus short-term projects* becomes important when there's a long-term web development effort going on concurrently with short-term changes to a web site. The essential point is that there are changes for the long term that overlap with changes for the short term, and the changes cannot go to production together. For this reason, the development efforts are split apart and done separately.

Rita's gang encounters the challenge of managing what essentially amounts to two distinctly different web properties. On one hand, there is an ongoing sequence of short-term changes to insert a new banner on the homepage, for which each takes only a few hours to go from implementation to approval. On the other hand, the deeper and more pervasive changes to integrate the third-party notification system take weeks to complete. The solution to this problem involves setting up separate "branches" of development, where each branch corresponds to a logically independent web site.

As the scope of the web operation expands, corporate marketing plays a larger role in directly creating content or sponsoring the creation of content by outside contributors, known as stringers. Nina, the corporate marketing manager, is an example of an inside contributor. When she assembles a press release, she focuses on the market positioning spin, the strategic sprinkling of third-party endorsements contained within the press release, and the go-live date of the release. At the same time, she defers to the art director's guidance on the layout of the press-release detail pages on the corporate site. The same goes for the choice of font for the title on the press-release summary page. Most of all, Nina appreciates that previously written press releases will be automatically reformatted to the current design rules.

Separating content from presentation is also known as *templating*.[3] The assets that comprise a web site must be factored in a way that allows many members of the web team to make changes concurrently. A content contributor is someone whose domain of responsibility focuses on the information content within a web site. Another department or group typically holds responsibility for determining the form of the presentation of the content. Because a large organization finds it essential to separate content from presentation, it centralizes art direction decisions, while it decentralizes content creation. This separation becomes more pronounced as an organization grows.

This is exactly what we see in this story. Nina, the corporate marketing manager, focuses on creating content. Divorcing the content from presentation lets her reuse content in many different situations, some of which was not anticipated when she created the content. For example, another manager uses a one-sentence summary of her piece as a caption on a promotional graphic. For Rita, the key is to design a content-capture framework that maximizes the opportunities for the content to be reused over its lifetime.

> By the middle of 2000, ezSuggestionBox.com expands its operations worldwide. Two regional development centers operate out of Boston and Chicago. To satisfy the customer traffic, production web farms operate in San Jose, Boston, Chicago, and London. The total asset base has grown to 500,000 web assets. Multiple content servers, geographically dispersed, host the assets.

The issue of *handling of very large-scale web sites* arises when web operations spread over development locations around the world, or when the volume of web assets exceeds the capacity of a single server to handle. Scalability of the software and hardware infrastructure is an essential consideration, regardless of the particular choice of technology.

In the case of ezSuggestionBox.com, the developers find the need to distribute assets among several content management servers when their operations expand into regional development centers. They reap the benefits from the fact that each development center uses a common infrastructure for content management and that the basic framework extends to handle future growth in assets.

---

[3] Chapter 5 discusses templating in greater detail.

Terminology

A *web property* is an aggregated presence on the World Wide Web with a single entry point, such as www.ezSuggestionBox.com or www.yahoo.com, or it is a disaggregated presence that is reached from multiple entry points, exemplified by banner ads hosted by doubleclick.net. One or more servers render a web property's presence on the Internet.

Web development encompasses creation, modification, review, and approval of assets. Examples of assets that we consider are web sites, source code repositories, document repositories, or any combination of these. Our focus is the development of assets. An individual or a group creates an asset, and it is costly, sometimes impossible to replace. A graphic file containing the company's logo is an asset. Similarly, a Java source code file that is used in an online commerce application server is also an asset.[4] The text of a press release or a product support bulletin is an asset. All of these embody intellectual property of an organization and are difficult or costly to replace.

Universality of Assets

When we speak about assets, it is sometimes tricky to distinguish a web asset from a nonweb asset. For example, a company's web banner logo graphic is easy to categorize as a web asset. On the other hand, it is more difficult to classify program code that contains an SQL query that extracts a customer's pending order that is invoked by an application server running in conjunction with a web server. Is that a web asset? We'll be pragmatic. If the logic or other intellectual property embodied in the program code affects the success of the web property, we'll consider it an asset within our area of concern. To emphasize the point, we'll refer to these as *extended web assets*. An extended web asset is directly or indirectly used to implement a web property. An extended web asset may not be a web asset in the strictest sense, but its ability to be developed in a timely and correct manner does affect the overall success of the web property. We'll use the shorter term, "asset," to refer to these extended web assets. For example, an automated voice-response telephony system uses prerecorded audio messages. Working in conjunction with a web property or working standalone, the audio message files are assets by our definition.

Web assets, we must emphasize, are passive. A web property comes alive through hardware and software that *renders* web assets. (See Figure 2.1.) For example, a "classical" web property renders HTML and images by using a combination of web server software running on stock hardware. The HTML and images constitute the web assets. Because web assets are passive, we store them, version them, index them, and

---

[4] Chapter 3 introduces the distinction between a source asset and a derived asset. For example, a Java source file is a source asset, while a compiled Java class file is a derived asset.

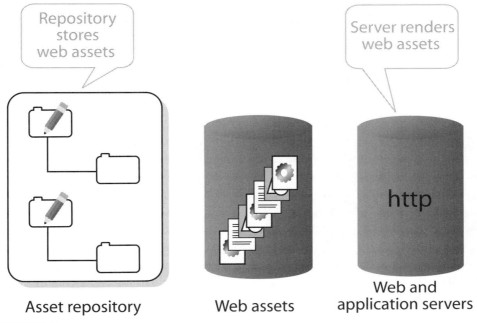

FIGURE 2.1
A repository stores assets while a server renders them to bring them to life.

retrieve them. In spite of their passivity, web assets define the essence of a web property. As such we must carefully protect and care for web assets by storing them in a content repository. (Paradoxically, the hardware and software to render assets consist of standard replaceable components: off-the-shelf computers and shrink-wrapped software components.)

The distinction between web assets and the rendering of web assets is critical; it underscores the proposition that the enterprise of web development focuses on creating and managing web assets. The fundamental challenge of content management is to protect and care for the web assets that give life to its web property.

Organizations choose varying approaches to rendering their web assets. One company chooses a traditional approach of HTML files, image files, augmented with CGI scripts. Another chooses a database-driven content server. Another devises a hybrid solution that combines a database-driven content server with a Java servlet-driven application server. Common application servers include products from IBM, Art Technology Group, BEA Systems, BroadVision, and Vignette. All of these mechanisms represent different approaches to the problem of rendering web assets. This idea extends to assets that implement extensions to the web server (such as Microsoft Active Server Pages) as well as assets hosted on the web server but downloaded into the client browser (such as Java applets). Content management transcends the specific choice of rendering technology. The requirement to manage the assets, preferably in some kind of repository, is universal across all the approaches.

Managing Web Assets

Web development groups change rapidly, especially the successful ones. They hire more staff. Teams tackle business objectives that expand and transform over time. The pace is relentless. Above all, the size of the operation tends to grow quickly. (See Figure 2.2.) Sometimes the business grows. The operation grows as fast as people can be hired, or the operation expands as it validates its business model.

As the size of the web operation increases, different techniques for managing the web property come into play. As we'll see, each technique overcomes important problems faced during development. Each technique has advantages and limitations.

In the following sections, we'll introduce four approaches to managing assets for a web property. The first one is suitable for a small web site consisting of fewer than a hundred assets. The others make sense for successively larger web operations, up through enterprise-class web sites with millions of assets.

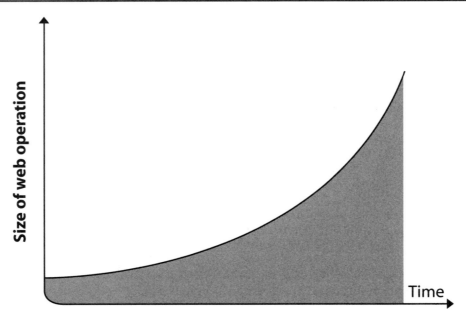

FIGURE 2.2
Web operations tend to grow rapidly.

Live Editing

For a very small web site produced by one or two developers, where the site consists of fewer than 100 files, it is common for the developers to edit the live web site directly. (See Figure 2.3.) The approach is simple. There is one copy of the web site, the live production copy. To make a change, edit the asset directly.

Since small web sites are typically exploratory efforts, uptime isn't essential. The number of hits on the web is small, and the fact that files may be temporarily missing or incorrect on the production web site doesn't affect many visitors. In Rita's story, live editing is adequate in the early days when her primary goal is to establish a proof of concept, during her "2 A.M. software" era.

This arrangement has the advantage of being simple to administer. Fix what needs to be fixed. Visit the live site to see if the site works. This simple scheme works because the entire site is under one person's management, and the live site is the latest working copy of the site.

The major disadvantage of this arrangement is that there is little control of the site. Typically, the only version control consists of making an entire copy of the web site occasionally. If a problem is discovered, and there's a need to revert some of the site, or the entire site to a previous working version, the copies are examined to determine which copy to roll back to.

Directly making changes on the production site has other unfortunate consequences. First, the solution doesn't scale on a number of dimensions. Only a handful of people can work on a live production site if a mistake becomes visible to the user base. This makes it impossible to accomplish objectives more rapidly by boosting staffing. Since the site must be fully functioning at all times, this severely limits the kinds of projects that can be undertaken. Any kind of change that requires multiple files to change in a coordinated fashion, or that require any testing at all, cannot be undertaken on a live site.

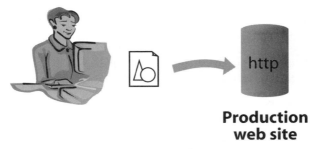

Production web site

FIGURE 2.3
Developers on small sites often edit the live web site directly.

Finally and perhaps most insidious, live editing promotes a self-limiting work culture that impedes future expansion. By its nature, live editing encourages a "web cowboy" mentality that hinders future development. One example is the ability of different production web servers to host a web property without rewriting the internal references. For example, if the web property of a hypothetical firm, the General Bot Corporation, uses fully qualified references, such as "href=http://www.generalbot.com/privacypolicy.html," then this limits the ability to test the web assets before moving them into production. Suppose for instance, that the company evaluates competing web-hosting vendors to more economically and reliably serve the corporate web site. This requires copying a snapshot of the web property to a test server to measure how different server configurations handle simulated loads. In our example, we want the test web server to handle the reference to the privacy policy, instead of unconditionally redirecting the viewer to the main corporate site. Internal references relative to the "docroot" should be made to "href=/privacypolicy.html" instead. This more closely expresses the true intent of the reference. The practice of live editing tends to mask the distinction between internal and external references, which impedes future expansion of the development team and the testing effort.

Staging the Web Site

As the number of assets grows, and the number of developers increases, it is no longer practical to edit the production web server directly. Enter a separate web server, or staging server. It runs a copy of the production web site, with the difference that we copy changes that the developers intend to put into production on the staging web server first. (See Figure 2.4.) This solution works on sites up to 1,000 assets, when the number of developers is less than five.

The staging web site solution is adequate when Rita's gang consists of a handful of developers. In the story, we see that as the efforts of the developers begin to take divergent paths, managing the changes and the testing within a single staging web site has significant limitations.

The staging server introduces the important ability to test changes before they go live. Developers are able to detect errors before they reach the production site. This solution is similar to the live edit procedure, except that developers point their browser at the staging server, instead of at the production server. As long as the number of developers is less than five or so, then the improvement in the ability to test outweighs the additional burden of the two-step procedure. First, move changes to the staging server. Second, copy the changes to the production server.

This solution begins to break down as the number of developers increases beyond a handful. With more developers, it becomes harder to keep track of individual changes. That trap befell Rita's organization in the opening story. Although Rita's development organization deserves credit for having progressed to a level of maturity where they recognize the importance of testing web content before going live, they

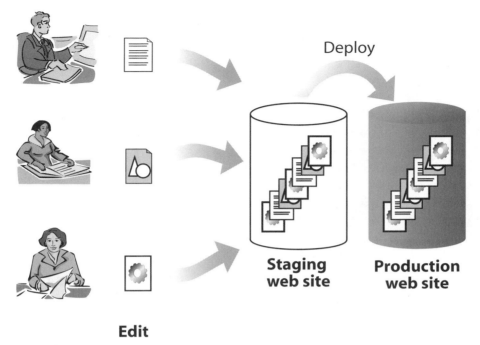

Deploy

Staging web site

Production web site

Edit

FIGURE 2.4

Copying a modified asset to a staging web site allows a development team to test changes before deploying them to the production web site.

are encountering the principal limitation with the staging server model. Their development team has too many members for each person to understand which changes belong to whom, and which changes are or are not ready to go into production.

Independent Edit Areas

At the next level of sophistication, development groups retain the staging server, but proceed to give each developer an independent area in which to make and test their changes. (See Figure 2.5.) This partially solves the problem of developers stepping on one another because each developer has a web server and a separate area in which to make their changes. This has the additional benefit that each developer is able to test changes independently. This approach has some amount of success with development teams up to eight, with number of assets fewer than 2,000 to 5,000.

Rita's band of renegades find the independent edit areas approach useful when they branch out into small project teams working on different assets. Keeping an accurate

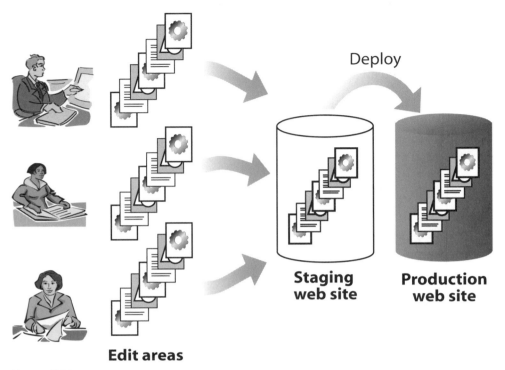

Deploy

**Staging
web site**

**Production
web site**

Edit areas

FIGURE 2.5
Developers on larger sites use separate edit areas to make and test changes.

version history is important, however, and it is wise to use this technique in conjunction with source code versioning tools.[5]

There are two drawbacks to this approach. First, as the number of independent areas increases to accommodate the developers, the total space consumed in the file system for each copy of the assets increases. Second, conflicts between areas become harder to keep track of. This happens because, with many developers, the likelihood of two people changing the same file increases. Let's suppose that two developers need to change index.html. One of them completes their change, and copies their change into the staging server. Assistance from a version control or content management tool is required to make a second developer aware that the changes to index.html are now

---

[5] A limitation of source-code versioning tools is that a person who isn't a software developer typically finds such tools difficult to use. The result is either frustration on the part of the developer, or a frequent "forgetfulness" in using the tool. Both are detrimental to the organization.

in conflict with the latest version of `index.html`. Without this kind of assistance, it is very likely that the second developer will overwrite the `index.html` in the staging server with their modified version of `index.html`. This effectively overwrites the changes from the first developer.

Content Management

When the asset count exceeds 2,000 to 5,000 files, or the web team exceeds 10–12 content developers and code developers, then it usually becomes necessary to adopt a content management tool. Formal support from a content management system overcomes the drawbacks of informal solutions, such as the ones described earlier. *Content management* is a discipline that manages the timely, accurate, collaborative, iterative, and reproducible development of a web property. (See Figure 2.6.) It combines a mechanism to store a collection of web assets with processes that seamlessly mesh the activities of people and machines within an organization. Content management responds to the unique combination of problems posed by web development.

Rita's gang should reasonably expect to support their activities with a content management approach by the time their group size reaches 12. If they allow time to evaluate, purchase, and implement such a system, and if they consider their rapid growth, they could reasonably start the process when their team is 8–10 people, depending on their hiring rate.

Since web efforts tend to expand quickly, both in terms of number of assets and size of staff, it often makes sense to introduce formal content management well in advance of crossing the asset and team size threshold suggested earlier. As rule of thumb, you should initiate the introduction of content management before your effort crosses the file count and team size thresholds, say, six months in advance. This gives time to evaluate tools, solicit budgetary approval, complete the purchase, implement the tool set, and train your staff, before the need becomes so critical that the absence of a content management solution impacts your business. In addition, the overall training cost

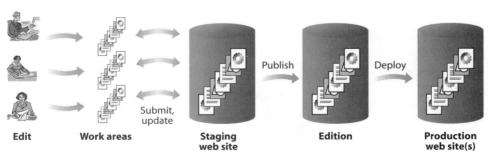

FIGURE 2.6
Content management orchestrates the development, testing, review, and deployment of web assets.

is lower if you introduce content management techniques when your staff is smaller, and fewer people become entrenched in bad habits.

Content Management Architecture

A content management infrastructure consists of subsystems that fulfill the following four functions (See Figure 2.7.):

- Content creation and editing
- Content repository and versioning
- Workflow and routing
- Deployment and operations management

Content Creation/Editing Subsystem

The content creation/editing subsystem consists of content editing tools, such as HTML editors, word processors, image editors, and XML editors. A wide variety of tools reflects the fact that each kind of content specialist, such as an artist creating an illustration or a telephone support associate creating a trouble ticket, becomes most efficient when that individual uses a tool suited to his or her expertise and problem domain. The job of the creation/editing subsystem is to accept input, effect appropriate processing on the input such as error checking, bounds checking, and whenever possible present direct feedback to tool users about the results of their actions. For

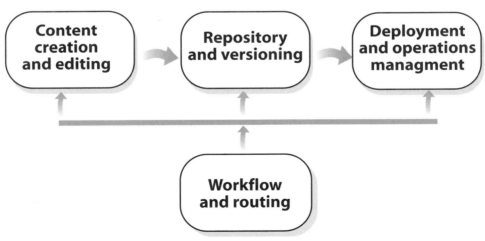

FIGURE 2.7
Four major subsystems of content management infrastructure.

example, developers creating servlets by writing Java code should see the effects of their code changes on an application server, preferably in real-time. We measure effectiveness of the creation/editing subsystem by the productivity of the content specialists that the subsystem serves. In addition, we can expect that the ability to support metadata tagging, using standard mechanisms such as XML, will become increasingly important.

Repository Subsystem

The repository subsystem provides storage, access, retrieval, indexing, versioning, and configuration management of content. Content includes files, database assets, and structured assets (e.g., XML). Access to content is available through standard means, including file system access, standard database access API's (ODBC, JDBC), and browser interface. We measure effectiveness of the repository subsystem according to its ability to store assets reliably, with scalability and with excellent performance.

Workflow Subsystem

The workflow subsystem manages assignments, routes jobs, handles notification to tie together the activities of the many specialists required to create, edit, test, review, and approve the plethora of simple and composite asset types in the repository. This subsystem needs to be aware of the content repository to allow job actions to be driven from repository changes, and conversely to have job actions to cause repository changes. Job specifications may be predefined statically, or ad hoc jobs may be created dynamically according to a "wizard" interface. The effectiveness of the workflow subsystem is measured by it ability to sustain work throughput, while offering simple means to define, modify, and specify new kinds of job routings.

Deployment and Operations Management

The deployment and operations management subsystem copies a variety of asset types from the development environment to production. It does so efficiently and reliably. Operation is 24×7. There needs to be simple mechanisms to provide positive assurance when systems work properly, and immediate notification and escalation when it detects an error state. Because operations often span the globe, crossing organization boundaries and multiple time zones, administration needs to be simple to set up, easy to learn, and provide detailed monitoring and audit trails. The effectiveness of the deployment and operations subsystem is measured by the reliability and throughput of the service, while minimizing the administrative effort.

Summary

The story of Rita and her gang illustrates predictable issues that confront a web operator. A web site swells from a skunkworks effort tended by one person to an enterprise-wide web site supported and maintained by hundreds of contributors. Some tend to the web site full-time, such as a Java developer implementing core functionality. Others contribute on a more casual basis, such as a contract writer adding a promotional piece against a predefined template.

Beneath the surface clutter of events, the swirl of growth in staff, and the expanded role of the web site in the business, the web site has a lifecycle of its own. It has a predictable set of universal lifecycle issues related to content management. Savvy managers consider these issues. We can see these issues in the fictitious story of Rita and her gang.

We have seen how the development of very small web sites, ranging in size up through enterprise-class web sites, can be managed with different approaches. (See Figure 2.8.) For a very small site, especially one that has a single developer, it is common for editing to occur on the live site. At the next level of sophistication, introduce

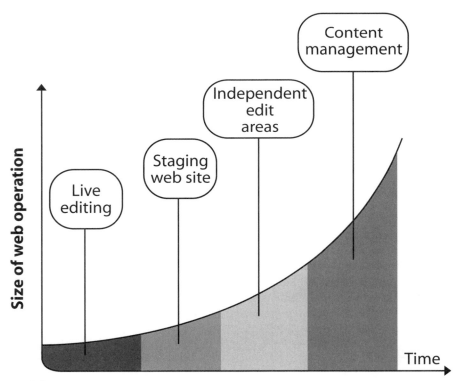

FIGURE 2.8
Choosing an approach to managing web assets depends on the size of your web operation.

a staging web site where one or more developers copy their changes for testing, review, and approval. For a larger team, or to support concurrent projects, introduce independent edit areas. Beyond 5,000 assets or a team of ten to twelve, it is highly recommended that a content management system be used.

Part Two

Concepts and Principles

CHAPTER THREE

PRINCIPLES OF COLLABORATIVE WEB DEVELOPMENT

Give us the tools and we will finish the job.* —*Winston Churchill*

Executive Summary

We introduce the basic principles of collaborative web development. They include identifying stakeholders, recognizing the Chaos Zone, distinguishing development and production phases of operation, identifying source assets, building direct feedback into work processes, exploiting parallel development, and performing both file and site-level versioning.

Introduction

Web development touches people, processes, assets, and tools. Building a content management infrastructure requires changes on all of these facets of the problem. You might think of these facets as being *fronts* in a campaign. On the people front, many parts of the organization contribute to the daily operations and set the direction for the web initiatives. On the process front, developing a web asset, whether it is Java code, an image, a logo, or business logic, has become complicated, because any single asset often sits at the confluence of technical, business, and organizational factors. No single person can do it all, and so many individual processes link complementary skills. On the assets front, a marketing manager writes a press release, but she doesn't define the artistic intent of the page layout. A Java developer writes code to query the inventory database, but someone else decides the policy that relates current stock levels to products to feature in the

41

*Speech on radio, February 9, 1941. In *Complete Speeches* vol 6, 1974, p.6350.

online store web property. On the tool front, specialists use desktop tools, web servers, and application servers to stitch together assets into a unified property.

Basic Concepts

Eight basic concepts form the foundation of content management practice. Each concept embodies a single technique or idea that plays a vital role in a comprehensive solution for content management.

- Identify stakeholders.
- Recognize the Chaos Zone.
- Separate development and production.
- Identify assets (source, derived, and deployed).
- Use direct feedback.
- Exploit parallel development.
- Use both file-versioning and site-versioning.
- Identify control mechanisms.

Stakeholder Identification

The cooperation of major stakeholders in the web operation is vital to successful implementation of a content management solution. A *stakeholder* is an individual or a group that either participates in the web development, deployment, or production processes, or is a sponsor of web initiatives. Sometimes stakeholders are even located outside your organization. The major stakeholders usually include the content contributor, the business owner, the content administrator, the production manager, and the executive. The diverse stakeholders have different needs and hold different perspectives that need consideration.

Each group of stakeholders benefits from an effective web development infrastructure in different ways. Occasionally, stakeholder groups work at cross-purposes. This adds an interesting dimension to our exposition. When we introduce a particular feature of the content management solution, we'll highlight the benefits derived by each stakeholder group.

The *web developer* needs a development environment and fast track to speed his or her intellectual contribution to the target audience. But at the same time, the developer's efforts should be fully supported with the checks and balances that only an organization can provide. Developers need to have their work reviewed both technically and from a business perspective, to have their work versioned, to have it tested. We'll define a web developer as a contributor who typically changes multiple web assets to complete a task.

The *content contributor* also needs a productive development environment. Unlike a web developer, a content contributor typically changes a single web asset. The content contributors also have a need for support in the form of technical and business-centric reviews of their work. They require effective testing and review of assets they contribute while rendering their work in a realistic context. Their contributions are highly structured; examples include artwork of precise shape and size, or highly structured, tagged text.

The *business owner* of a web initiative needs a way to express his or her priorities, with the ability to advise and comment to the end product as it moves through development. Does the content look right? Does it convey the right impression? The business owner cares that that the business goals are achieved, according to both tangible measures and intangible factors that require visual inspection. For example, a business goal might be to convey a seamless linkage from a company web site to a business partner's web site. To make this determination, the business owner of the company's partnership needs to grasp the physical layout of the page, and the "feel" and the placement of the required clicks.

The *content administrator* wants to assure that scarce company resources are applied effectively to manage and evolve the web property. The overall goal is to build a solid infrastructure so that all groups work effectively. In addition, the content administrator must make sure that the talent that took so much effort to recruit and retain is productive, and that busy-work and throwaway work are absolutely minimized. All assets need to be present and accounted for. Remember that the talent goes home at the end of the day, but the organization is responsible to manage and keep safe the fruits of everyone's daily labors, namely the web assets.

The *production manager* desires that the production version of the web property is of high quality, and that it moves to production to the correct location, at the right time. In addition, the web property must be resilient so that if a problem is found in the web property there is an immediately available backup copy. Since mistakes can occur at any time, there needs to be a prearranged way to revert to a last known-good copy of a web property.

The *business executive* wants infrastructure and processes to allow the business to react swiftly to changes, whether they are competitive pressures, market pressures, or simply the need to move quickly, surely, and with measured steps on a business initiative.

All of these stakeholders have needs that are vital to the successful operation of a web-based business. Any solution must take into account their needs and motivations. This is our first principle of content management.

Principle #1:
A content management solution must take into account the needs and motivations of the major stakeholders, including web developers, content contributors, business owners, content administrators, production managers, and executives.

Are We in the Chaos Zone?

"Hey, someone clobbered my changes!"

Although multiple people change an asset, this needn't be a problem if this conflict condition is detected and handled appropriately. Without this detection, one person's change can overwrite someone else's. The downfall is the inability to deal with multiple modifiers of the same asset, or possibly to preclude multiple modifiers in the first place.

"I didn't know that was changing!"

This is a milder form of the previous problem. The surprise reveals that some change should have been known. Someone should have been notified. A succession of surprises of this sort undermines the team's confidence in undertaking tasks with assurance. Occasionally the problem leads to loss of data.

"No single person can keep track of all the changes anymore."

This person wishes that a single person could keep track of all changes, but that's no longer practical. The problem is now out of hand. There's a sense of resignation. The organization must act quickly before morale suffers irreparably, or the business sustains damage.

"Hey, my change wasn't supposed to go out yet!"

Running a web site requires deft timing of deployments of time-sensitive or periodic events. This process is definitely out of control, because the content owner's change went live prematurely. Perhaps deployment procedures are error-prone. Perhaps content owners don't have a way to specify the required deployment timing on an asset. Perhaps content with different timing requirements is mixed together.

"I'm stuck, because your changes broke my stuff!"

When one person's change "breaks" someone else's, this reveals that there is inadequate integration of the changes. Who went first, or what broke what, isn't really the point. This is a process breakdown. The organization needs to take steps to strengthen the process and build an infrastructure that makes it natural for integration to occur. Encourage early and frequent integration of changes.

These signs indicate a realm that we refer to as the Chaos Zone. Managing a development effort becomes increasingly challenging when it enters this mode of operation. The Chaos Zone is defined when a web operation can be characterized as follows:

- More than 5,000 assets
- More than seven developers, reviewers, testers
- More than one deployment per week
- Scale of business exceeds $1 million annually

Although these figures should be interpreted as approximate guidelines, they are chosen to reflect the scale at which a web operation begins to experience the productivity-sapping effects of chaos. If three or more of these factors are true for your operation, then the content management solution recommended in this chapter should be seriously considered. As a web operation increases in size, pace, and importance, most organizations reach a point that existing informal processes and tools become inadequate for the challenge at hand.

Recognize the signs of the Chaos Zone. Existing processes are different. They become inadequate at different thresholds. For example, a web team might use the practice of making changes directly on the production web server, known as the "direct edit" approach. Another team might make their changes on a staging server and enlist the help of a small team of people to selectively copy changes to the production web server; this is known as the "staging server" approach. Each of these approaches has different advantages and drawbacks, relative to the approach that will be presented in this chapter. Regardless of the approach, the benefits of formal content management become especially dramatic in the Chaos Zone.

Development and Production Separation

Web development in the Chaos Zone involves large numbers of contributors, and the process must move quickly. Each day represents a seething chaotic mass of activity that has the potential to spin out of control without warning. With chaos a possible outcome, the final output from the activity is critical to the organization, and must be carefully controlled.

The primary goal of development is to arrange people and processes to efficiently and rapidly allow an organization to create, edit, review, and test successive changes to a web property. Development combines editorial, creative, and programming inputs to produce a released version. A *released version* of a web site is the complete set of web assets corresponding to a given point in time. We'll also refer to the released version as simply a *version* of a web site. Here we use the term web asset in a broad sense; a *web asset* is a file, a directory, or a row in a database table.

> *Principle #2:*
> Separate development activity by deploying controlled released versions of assets to production.

This principle divides the difficult job of managing a web property into two smaller subproblems: development and production. Usually a different organization manages development, compared to production. Deploying controlled, released versions of our web property defines a clear handoff between the two organizations. Deployment, shown in Figure 3.1, is discussed at greater length in Chapter 7.

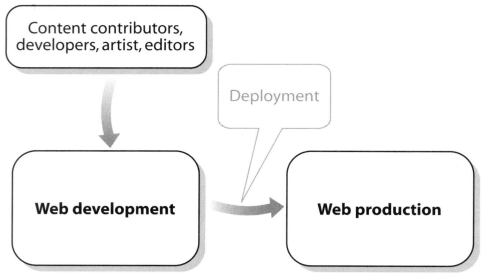

FIGURE 3.1

Deployment moves developed web assets to one or more production servers.

Asset Identification

Content management is all about managing, protecting, nurturing, and evolving an ever-increasing collection of assets in a web property. We retain previous versions of a web property. We often need previous versions as archival copies, as references to assist in ongoing development, or to retain the ability to revert an individual asset, or to revert an entire web property to a designated last known-good version.

Because they are entirely in digital form, assets can be copied, moved, manipulated, and transformed with ease, thanks to the help of powerful computers and storage devices. But storage capacity and processing power aren't limitless. The key to success is to save precisely what we need, but no more. We may retrieve some previous version of the entire web property, or one particular version of a specific asset contained within it.

If we save more than what is minimally required, we will eventually regret that choice. At least at first, storage capacity seems limitless, like the empty rooms of a house after you first move in. You're eager to fill the rooms with furniture. But like the house filled with clutter, a storage device filled with superfluous copies of assets becomes a burdensome chore to manage. Add to that the difficulty of finding what we're looking for. The same happens to a web property, as unnecessary historical copies add clutter, making it more difficult to find specific assets for specific dates.

Our task now is to define the minimal set of assets required to regenerate a web property. A *source asset* is a special category of asset that is valuable because it is the result of a skilled individual using a tool. We strive to maintain possession of this asset because its contents are difficult or impossible to reproduce. A *derived asset* is an asset that can be automatically generated through a tool or other automatic procedure, possibly from another asset. The property that distinguishes a source asset from a derived asset is that a derived asset can be easily reproduced, whereas a source asset cannot. For example, a Photoshop .psd file typically represents the work of a skilled artist, and if we were to lose a Photoshop file, it might be difficult or impossible to recreate the original image. In other words, a Photoshop .psd file is a source asset. In contrast, we consider a .gif file a derived asset when it can be regenerated from a source asset.

For the purposes of web content management, we version source assets. We reuse them, or use them to base follow-on work. For example, we put an Active Server Page (.asp) and a Java Server Page (.jsp) source file under version control. First, we may need to refer to the logic that it contains. Second, we revert to a previous version of the file if we discover a critical bug in the current version of the file. Third, we create an improved version of the file by using some previous version as the starting point.

Here's our third principle of web content management.

> *Principle #3:*
> Version all source assets.
>
> *Corollary:*
> A derived asset that isn't needed for rollback purposes needn't be versioned.

We'll see later that under certain circumstances deployed assets, including some derived assets, ought to be versioned as well.

Direct Feedback (WYSIWYG)

A web property's value depends on the experience that it provides for the user, on the visual elements, together with active elements and embedded logic that respond to requests, such as search and personalization engines. In the same way that a web visitor responds to a page layout or to the tactile feel of a mouse-over navigation element, the creator, tester, and reviewer most effectively and rapidly judge the suitability of those elements by experiencing them in the context of a functioning web site. Identical factors govern the experience of developing, testing, and reviewing the underlying assets in the first place. Here's our fourth principle.

> *Principle #4:*
> Use direct feedback to maximize the effectiveness of a web developer.

The direct feedback paradigm says that the activities within a work cycle should minimize the perceptual distance between making a change and viewing the results of the change—in other words, apply the *what-you-see-is-what-you-get principle* (*WYSIWYG*) to web assets. For example, change a common included navigation file; then view how the modified look affects the user experience throughout a web site.

Parallel Development

Multiple concurrent projects can mean you are in the Chaos Zone. At any single time, projects are commencing, some are in mid-flight, while others are in the completion phases of testing and review. This is inevitable given the size of the team, the number of assets, and the frequency of updates to the production web site.

In an environment with multiple concurrent projects, it is essential to provide ongoing tasks with separate copies of the web property so that each can make edits, test the result, and solicit review and approval. We define a *task* as a set of interrelated changes to the web property. Here are some examples of tasks.

   a. A single developer makes an HTML change.
   b. A web designer and a graphic designer collaborate on new pages.
   c. A developer changes the logic in C++ files to fix a bug.
   d. Several marketing managers create press releases, all of which are scheduled to go-live on the same day.

Notice that in the list items (a) and (c), a single developer uses a work area. (See Figure 3.2.) In items (b) and (d), several people work in the same work area. In (b), a web designer and a graphic artist collaborate on new pages, so in this case, it makes sense for them to work in the same work area because their changes don't interfere with each other's. For example, the web designer might change the HTML, while the artist might change the images. In example (d), the marketing managers make changes independently (Figure 3.3), but the commonality is that all of their changes go-live on the same day.

Arrange to conduct development on a single task in each work area. This is our fifth principle.

> *Principle #5:*
> Use a work area for a single task.

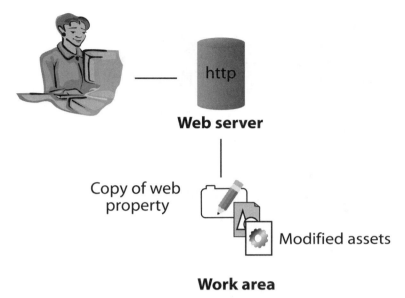

Web server

Copy of web property

Modified assets

Work area

FIGURE 3.2
A developer gets direct feedback from the results of her changes.

This typically means that each content contributor has a separate work area, or possibly a small handful of people working closely together use a common work area.[1] This minimizes the overlap and potential interference between the tasks.

Versioning

Versioning means that there are earlier versions to refer to, and that earlier versions are available to fall back to, as an insurance policy. Although mistakes always occur, people are more productive, daring, and innovative when they know that there is a safety net to rescue them.

---

[1] In practice, especially when one is developing application server assets, such as Java servlet or JSP assets, there is a tradeoff between providing each developer with his or her own instance of an application server, and having an entire group share a single instance. In this situation, we distinguish between "power developers" who affect critical server code and thereby routinely "crash" the web application during everyday development, and "normal developers" whose changes can safely coexist on the application server with other developers like themselves. A realistic compromise gives each power developer a dedicated application server instance, while groups of normal developers share a single application server instance.

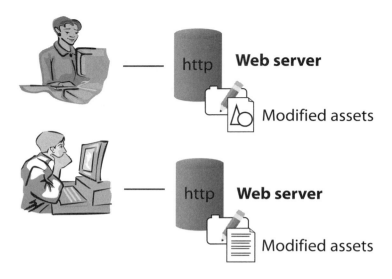

Separate work areas

FIGURE 3.3
Tasks proceed independently in separate work areas.

Content management relies on two kinds of versioning. *Submit* is a composite opera-tion that copies an asset from a work area to the staging area,[2] makes an immutable snapshot of the asset, records the current time and submitter, and collects a textual comment from the submitter. In *file-level versioning*, an asset is submitted to the stag-ing area when the asset has been tested and reviewed; it is now ready to be incorpo-rated into the work areas of other developers. Once in the staging area, a submitted asset is read-only in the following sense. It can only be superseded by a newer version from one of the work areas, or it can be deleted from the staging area.[3] The submis-sion of an asset is an important event, because subsequent testing and review takes place on a fixed copy of an asset.

Publish is a composite operation that creates a read-only copy of the entire web stag-ing area, records the current time and publisher, and collects a textual comment from

---

[2] The staging-area paradigm can be simulated by a version control system, by a software configuration management system, or by a smart file system that supports the paradigm directly. The smart file system is described in greater detail in Appendix A.

[3] As we'll see in the next chapter, it is safe to "delete" an asset because judicious use of the "publish" opera-tion retains deleted assets in the per-file and per-site version history.

the publisher. In *site-level versioning*, the current content of the staging area is published as an edition. This operation records an edition, which is an immutable snapshot of the contents of the staging area. The read-only snapshots of the staging area become known reference points on which subsequent development is based.

File and site-level versioning encourages multiple streams of work conducted in parallel, whereas file and site versioning operations record the contents of assets individually or as an entirety. Versioning boosts productivity and throughput because developers make changes confidently, knowing that previous asset versions provide a safety net in case of a misstep.

Control Mechanisms: Auditing and Enforcement

The size of an organization strongly influences auditing and enforcement requirements. *Auditing* records the results of important activities, such as submitting a file or deploying changes to production. *Enforcement* is an activity that allows and denies the ability to carry out key activities, such as reading a file, modifying a file, changing a field in a data record, or deploying content to a particular production server during a certain time period.

To illustrate these concepts, we'll introduce three broad categories of human organizations—a tribe, a chiefdom, and a state.[4] As you will see, these will serve as metaphors for types of web development organizations. Distinguished mainly by size, each kind of organization adopts particular ways of communicating within itself, making decisions, and influencing the behavior of its members.

A *tribe* consists of a small, tightly knit group of people. In a tribe everybody knows everyone else, and information flows freely. Despite the presence of a tribal leader, decision-making tends to be informal or even communal. In a tribe, consensus tends to be an important part of the decision-making process. There is minimal process or bureaucracy. If we extend this idea to the context of web development, an organization with tribe-like characteristics focuses on moving quickly and safely. This means that work routing and version control are strong needs. Communication within the tribe tends to be effective. Because of the level of trust and communication, permission systems, access control, formal authorization and auditing aren't necessary.

A *chiefdom* consists of a group of people who have exceeded the ability of tribe-like behaviors to suit their needs. Too large for free-flowing informality, a chiefdom installs a chief to initiate jobs that carry out the chief's intentions. Specialization

---

[4] Jared Diamond, *Guns, Germs, and Steel: The Fates of Human Societies*, W.W. Norton & Co., New York and London, 1999, p. 270.

occurs within functional areas. However, since this specialization doesn't negate the need for information to continue to flow between areas, there's an important need to gather, record, and pass information between functional areas. Despite the criticality of information flow, there's a countervailing need to control the flow of certain kinds of information, and to restrict the flow of other kinds of information. Most of the operation remains informal, but assistant chiefs or trusted tribal members are given additional latitude. They become the "glue" that makes the loosely organized system work.

We can extend this idea to web development. With the larger number of members, a chiefdom cannot be as informal or freewheeling as a tribe. There's a need to track the activities of members. A chiefdom institutes audit mechanisms to record important activities, such as deploying new content to the production servers. In case something goes wrong, audit trails enable the group to determine the cause and to provide a remedy. It is important to note that the ability to audit does not itself prevent intentional misbehavior nor does it preclude accidents. Instead, social pressures are sufficient to encourage good behavior, without resorting to heavy-handed enforcement.

A *state* stands in contrast to a tribe or chiefdom in that a significant amount of collective energy focuses on making normal activities uniform and predictable. Although a state has more resources at its disposal, because of its scale, it has little ability to bestow blanket trust on significant segments of its populace with certain knowledge or certain capabilities. Instead, it expends effort to deny certain knowledge and capabilities to defined segments, and to enforce such restrictions in a provable manner. A state relies on enforcement. It has exceeded the scale at which simple trust is sufficient, as in a tribe.

In a web development context a *state* consists of a group of people so large that no single person or even group of trusted individuals can make it all work. Distinct functions have evolved each with a defined charter. There's a continual effort to refine and redefine department charters. It is an ongoing struggle to codify practices and disseminate knowledge in order to repeat successes and to avoid mistakes of the past. The flow of information is more strictly controlled. There's a need to meet audit requirements, for instance, to prove that so-and-so did something, or conversely to be able to prove that so-and-so could not possibly have done something. Rules and regulations prevent unauthorized access to forbidden resources, and block the ability to initiate a prohibited action.

A state thus exceeds the ability of simple auditing of key activities to achieve its goals. A state's larger population contains both newcomers and old-timers who aren't fully aware of carefully honed rules and regulations. Practicality dictates that a state clearly defines responsibilities and capabilities, and that the use of rights to exercise those capabilities be enforced, instead of merely audited.

We see then that the size of an organization imposes constraints on the mechanisms at its disposal to carry out its activities. A tribe has the luxury to adopt informal procedures and consensus decision making. A chiefdom relies more heavily on functional specialization and wide-scale communication becomes less efficient. Auditing is essential. In addition, a chiefdom relies on social pressures to avoid enforcement as a tool. A state, just by virtue of its scale, can no longer rely on social pressures and auditing. Instead, enforcement becomes essential. Make no mistake, enforcement adds necessary overhead, such as adding a group to administer access controls, or requiring that a deployment script check that the initiator has the proper authorization before commencing the deployment itself.

We can extend the tribe-chiefdom-state idea as we analyze an online issue such as knowledge of the root or administrator password. In a tribe, each member is trusted to use the root password in a responsible manner. The practical reality is that everyone at some time or another will need to use it, and everyone is trusted to use that knowledge and capability wisely. If an unintended consequence or misuse occurs, the tribe gathers to pool their collective knowledge to identify and repair the breach.

In a chiefdom, most people don't need to know the root password, but it is common knowledge because there's a loosely organized substructure that routinely needs to use it. If some activity needs the root password, everyone is but a handful of steps away from someone who possesses that knowledge. Efficiency has higher precedence over precise control.

In a state, authority must be granted for critical information, such as to know and use the root password to selected job functions. It is important to prove that large segments cannot possibly know, and therefore cannot possibly misuse the root password. Any breach of this rule is itself a problem, because the state loses its ability to eliminate certain possibilities if a problem were to occur. By this line of reasoning, it follows that someone must have explicit responsibility to deny root password access to nearly everyone in the state.

This discussion applies to other access and capabilities as well: for example, the ability to see or change a file in a certain area of the web site, or the ability to deploy specific content to a particular production server at a certain time.

Table 3.1 shows a checklist to categorize the character of an organization. Knowing this, it is possible to infer the issues and requirements that will be important to that organization, and thereby know how to focus the implementation effort.

TABLE 3.1
Characteristics of Organizations and Their Control Mechanisms

Organization	Characteristics	Control Mechanism	Examples
Tribe	1. Small, tightly-knit group 2. Everyone knows everyone else. 3. Information flows freely.	Informal, consensus-driven	1. In the interest of expediency, everyone knows the root password. 2. Everyone is trusted to "do the right thing" when it comes to deploying updated content to production servers.
Chiefdom	1. Chief initiates major actions. 2. Specialization within functions 3. Less unstructured communication between functional areas 4. Assistants to chief act as information conduits between functional areas.	Auditing, together with social pressure, promotes proper behavior.	1. Analyze mistakes by use of logs. 2. Keep track of who deployed, what was deployed, when it was done, etc.
State	1. Functions have formal charters. 2. Significant efforts to codify practices and disseminate knowledge 3. Formal rules define proper behavior. 4. Rights and responsibilities are formally defined for job functions.	Enforcement of formally defined rights and privileges required.	1. Maintain explicit list of who is allowed to deploy, and what each person (or group) is allowed to deploy. 2. Before deploying, check that initiator of deployment is permitted to perform operation.

Summary

We've described the following basic concepts of web content management:

- Identify stakeholders.
- Recognize the Chaos Zone.
- Distinguish development and production phases of operation.
- Identify source assets.
- Build direct feedback into work processes.
- Support parallel development.
- Perform file and site-level versioning.
- Identify the organization's control mechanisms.

Each concept will be used as a building block in the next chapter as part of an integrated content management solution.

CHAPTER FOUR

BEST PRACTICES FOR COLLABORATIVE WEB DEVELOPMENT

"Make this awful thing stop!" ordered Mr. Teavee.

"Can't do that," said Mr. Wonka. "It won't stop till we get there. I only hope no one's using the other elevator at this moment."

"What other elevator?" screamed Mrs. Teavee.

"The one that goes the opposite way on the same track as this one," said Mr. Wonka.

"Holy mackerel!" cried Mr. Teavee. "You mean we might have a collision?"

"I've always been lucky so far," said Mr. Wonka.

—Roald Dahl,
Charlie and the
Chocolate
Factory.

57

Executive Summary

The fundamental problem of web development is to rapidly and precisely produce changes that are responsive to business needs. The goal is to efficiently organize people, processes, and tools around the assets of a web property. To achieve that organization, one must assign the tasks of creating, editing, reviewing, and testing assets to diverse specialists, who produce finished web assets to be deployed to production. An effective web development environment maximizes the throughput of changes to the web property while maintaining control of the process and the content.

The WSE Paradigm

One of the hard-won lessons we have gained from helping development groups implement more robust systems and procedures is that building an effective collaboration environment rests on clear roles and responsibilities. And whereas software tools help to facilitate the process and to automate certain tasks, development is fundamentally a collaborative social process.

With that in mind, we're going to proceed on two fronts. On the one hand, we're going to introduce and define a particular style of organization of individual and shared work products, and also introduce a set of basic collaboration operations. This organization forms the technical underpinning for a content management system. Then we'll interpret the meaning of the various operations within a social context of collaboration.

These two views are no different from the ways that we interpret a corner stop sign. At the technical level of interpretation, a stop sign tells us to bring our vehicle to a complete halt, under the threat of a traffic ticket if we are caught in violation. At the social level of interpretation, there's a tacit agreement between drivers at an intersection that fewer accidents and injuries result if drivers agree to stop and look both ways before proceeding through. By analogy, the content management system defines the "rules of the road," but ultimate success and satisfaction will derive from understanding the intent of the rules, and following them wisely.

We call the collaboration approach the *"WSE" paradigm*, shorthand for "work area/ staging area/edition" paradigm. WSE relies on multiple work areas, a single staging area, and some editions (versions of the web property); these organize the flow and integration of changes from developers. (See Figure 4.1.) The previous chapter introduced the notion of a *work area*, which is an independent copy of the web property that is used to add, remove, and modify assets. The use of multiple work areas fosters parallel development of many tasks. Multiple work areas have the desirable effect of increasing the rate at which projects complete, by giving each developer a controlled work environment.

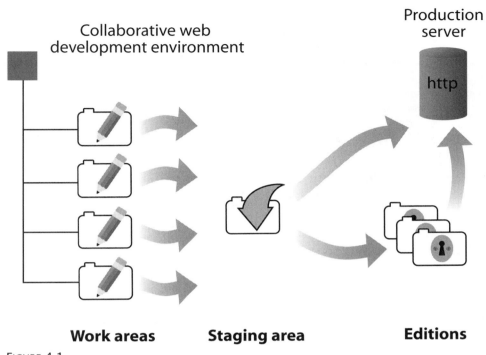

Work areas   Staging area   Editions

FIGURE 4.1
The WSE paradigm uses work areas, staging areas, and editions to organize the flow of changes from development to production.

Eventually the new and modified assets need to be brought together. This blend occurs in a single *staging area*. The staging area is like a work area because it too contains a copy of the web property, but it is different because it accepts changes from a work area (the staging area through the incorporation of new, modified, and deleted[1] assets). This file-level versioning operation captures a copy of the asset and records the submitter, the work area, the submission time, and comments.

Collaboration Strategies

In a collaborative development environment, each developer works on a task in a work area. Depending on the overlap between her work and the work of others, the developer must be vigilant for changes submitted by her colleagues as she submits

---

[1] An asset is removed from the staging area by "submitting a deletion."

changes to the staging area. Four collaboration modes are depicted in the graph shown in Figure 4.2. The most effective integration of the incoming flow of changes depends on the nature of the collaboration among colleagues.

The horizontal dimension in Figure 4.2 indicates whether assets are primarily new, or whether changes are primarily to existing assets. On one hand, the changes being made by a developer can consist primarily of new assets. For example, a contributor can create new assets, such as a writing a press release or building a new section of a web site. On the other hand, changes might involve mostly modifications to existing assets. For example, someone might be assigned to modify elements on an index page, or to add a question and answer to the frequently-asked-question page.

The vertical dimension in Figure 4.2 indicates whether one or many people are making changes to assets of the task at one time. For example, the frequently-asked-

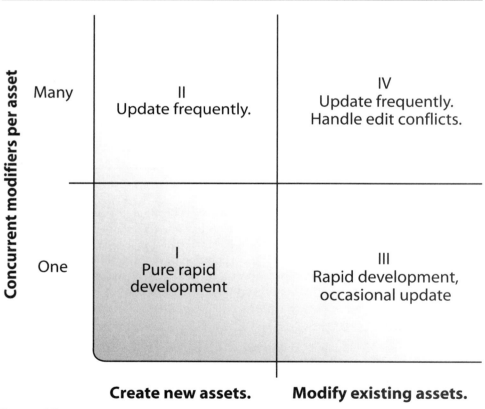

FIGURE 4.2
The activity type and the number of concurrent modifiers determines the best development strategy.

question page may not be actively changed, so that there's at most one person making a change at a given time. On the other hand, because the index page typically functions as a gateway into major sections of a web site, an index page tends to have people attempting to update the same page.

When we overlay these two dimensions on a graph, we get four quadrants; these describe the most effective strategies to moving changes efficiently to production. In quadrant I, because assets are primary new ones, and because the assets are relatively isolated and infrequently changed by others, there is little chance for collision. Focusing purely on rapid development is the best strategy.

In quadrant II, assets are primarily new, but the section of the web site has assets that are frequently changed by others. In this case, the best strategy is to develop rapidly, but to be cognizant of the changes made by others. This could mean frequent updates, or developers receiving notification when changes occur in the staging area.

In quadrant III, changes are primarily made to existing assets, and the changes are relatively isolated. Because the likelihood of collision is low, the best strategy is to develop rapidly, with occasional updates or notification to stay apprised of impending collisions.

In quadrant IV, modifications occur in existing assets and the likelihood of simultaneous edits on the same asset is frequent. In this situation, the challenges of carefully orchestrating the efforts of the development team are especially great.

Collaboration Operations

Five basic collaboration operations govern the movement of assets from a work area; moving them into the common stage area; comparing, updating, and merging assets so as to integrate changes from other work areas; to, finally publishing an edition. These operations are shown in Table 4.1. Each operation is much more than merely copying a web asset from one place to another. For example, the movement of assets from a work area that is typically used by a single developer into the staging area that is shared by all affects the entire team. Just as we cannot help but interpret graffiti placed on a highway overpass as having a larger social meaning, each submission of an asset into the staging area makes an important social statement to the organization. The contents of the staging area represent common assets for the organization, and small changes can have a major impact. For instance, two days before a major release, a developer wisely decides to delay submitting "clean-up" Java servlet code consisting of renaming variables, reordering the subroutines, and reformatting the indent structure of the code. Success of the release depends on knowing precisely which old problems have been fixed and being able to isolate sources of new problems by focusing closely on recently changed logic. Development is collaborative, and a developer must always recognize the larger social context of the development effort.

TABLE 4.1
Basic Collaboration Operations

Operation	Description	Interpretation
Submit	Copy assets from work area to staging area.	"To my esteemed colleagues, I have completed, tested, and have obtained approval for the following assets. They are suitable for integration into your ongoing work."
Compare	Compare assets in work area with corresponding assets in staging area.	"I am at a point in the work on my task that I'd like to see the new and modified assets in the staging area, for possible integration into my work area."
Update	Copy assets from staging area to work area.	"I believe that updating my work area with the following assets will help me stay in closer synchronization with recently submitted changes from my colleagues, and hence enhance my ability to submit my changes when that time comes."
Merge	Resolve conflict between staging area and work area.	"I've modified an asset for which another colleague has also modified and has submitted. To keep this asset synchronized with the staging area, and to enhance my ability to submit my modifications later, I will merge selected changes from the staging area's copy into my copy of this asset."
Publish	Create edition, which is a snapshot of entire staging area.	"The staging area comprises a version of our web property that will be useful to us, either as a distinguished snapshot in time (such as an archival reference), or a potential rollback version of our web property. As such, I'm creating this edition."

Table 4.1 shows two main ideas. First, it describes five basic collaboration operations—submit, compare, update, merge, publish—and describes them in terms of the movement of assets between areas. Second, and more significantly, the table suggests an interpretation of each action in a larger social context of collaboration.

Submit Operation

Submitting an asset from a work area, as shown in Figure 4.3, presents the asset to the rest of the organization. It is more than a developer claiming, "I'm done." Instead, inserting the new or modified asset into the staging area is merely the first hand-off step in integrating the asset into the web property. With it goes a presumption that the asset has been sufficiently tested and reviewed, and therefore is suitable to be

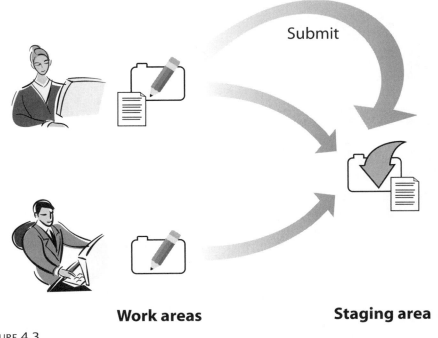

Work areas   **Staging area**

FIGURE 4.3
A developer submits her changes to the staging area.

---

integrated into the ongoing work of the rest of the organization. A healthy organization demonstrates mutual respect by adhering to the convention that submitted assets are high quality, as demonstrated by explicit testing and peer reviews.

Compare Operation

The *compare* operation identifies new, modified, and deleted assets in the staging area, with respect to a given work area. For example, a second developer might compare his work area to the contents of the staging area (Figure 4.4). The possible comparison results are shown in Table 4.2. This gives a developer the opportunity to decide which differences to pull into his work area. The comparison reveals a mixture of internal changes made within the work area and external changes that have been submitted to the staging area by others. If external changes have a reputation for high quality, the developer will feel more confidence in readily pulling in changes. In the compare-update work cycle, certain specific differences might need to be resolved.

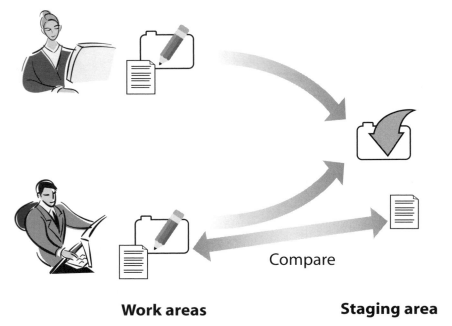

Work areas   **Staging area**

FIGURE 4.4
A second developer compares his work area to the contents of the staging area.

TABLE 4.2
Possible Comparison Results between Work Area and Staging Area

Case	Description	Conflict	Possible Actions
1	Same version as in staging area	No	None
2	Modified, based on version currently in staging area	Yes	Submit change from work area. Revert to previous version in staging area. Merge changes into work area's asset.
3	Modified, based on different version than currently in staging area	Yes	Merge work area with staging. Overwrite staging to override conflict and submit work area's asset. Force update workarea to overwrite the work area asset with asset from staging area.
4	Deleted in work area, exists in staging area	No	Submit deletion to remove asset in staging area. Force update work area to undo the deletion in work area.

Table 4.2
Possible Comparison Results between Work Area and Staging Area (Continued)

Case	Description	Conflict	Possible Actions
5	New in work area, no corresponding asset in staging area	No	Submit change from work area. Force update work area to discard new asset.
6	New in staging area, no corresponding asset in work area	No	Update work area to pull change from staging area into work area. Overwrite submit deletion to delete the asset from the staging area.

Update Operation

Update is the collaboration operation that copies changes from the staging area into a given work area (Figure 4.5). When changes have consistently high quality, frequent updates to ongoing development are beneficial to the organization as a whole.

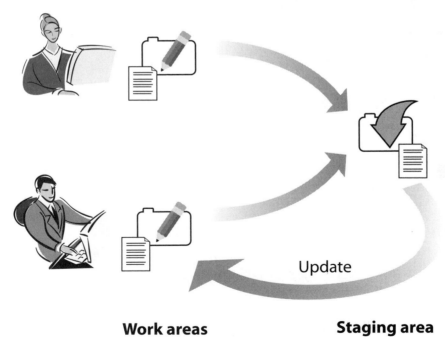

Work areas   **Staging area**

Figure 4.5
Changes in the staging area that haven't been modified in the work area can be updated into the work area.

Smaller, incremental updates with controlled disruptive effect spread the burden of integration over a longer period. This avoids costly one-time disruptions.

Merge Operation

Merge is the collaboration operation that resolves conflicts between a workarea and the staging area. (See Figure 4.6.) This takes care of changes that require more than just copying in. It is an essential part of achieving maximum productivity because conflicts need resolution before submission. Merging incrementally during development, instead of deferring all merges until the last moment, typically takes less time and produces less aggravation.

Publish Operation

An important collaboration operation is *publish*, which records a snapshot of the staging area as shown in Figure 4.7.

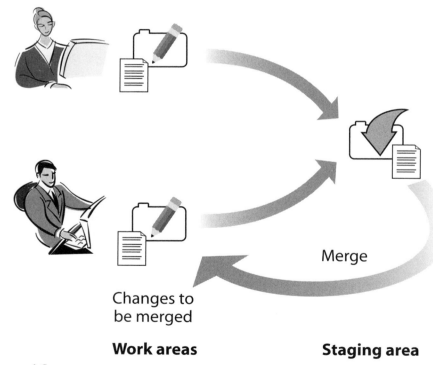

Work areas   **Staging area**

FIGURE 4.6
Merging a change resolves the conflict with a previously submitted asset.

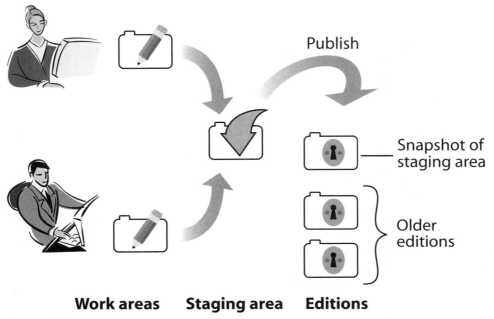

Work areas   Staging area   Editions

FIGURE 4.7
Publishing an edition creates a whole-site snapshot of the staging area.

The key is to strike a balance between the raw speed of development and the need to stay synchronized with changes made by others. These are two important factors that impinge on the development process, and it is important to take them into account when designing the content management infrastructure.

Work Cycles

Another important concept is the notion of a work cycle. A *work cycle* is a sequence of development steps related to creating, editing, testing, and reviewing assets. It often culminates in a feedback opportunity for a developer. Is the work ready for the next steps, or does it need to travel through the work cycle once again? The feedback helps determine what occurs next.

Identifying work cycles in the web development process is important because the time that people spend in one cycle or another accounts for the bulk of the total effort. For this reason, shortening the duration of the basic work cycles boosts the overall productivity. Direct feedback plays an essential role in keeping work cycles short. There are typically four important work cycles in a web development environment, which we describe in more detail in the next section.

In an effective development environment, mechanisms and procedures are instituted to minimize the elapsed time for each work cycle. Direct feedback minimizes the elapsed time of a work cycle by tightly coupling a change with the feedback from the change.

Version Snapshots

Handoff from one person to the next occurs as a transition between work cycles. It is a good practice to take a version snapshot at the completion of a work cycle. This serves two purposes. First, it leaves an audit trail. Second, and perhaps more importantly, asset versioning provides the ability to isolate problems, and to roll back to earlier versions of specific assets if needed.

> *Principle #6:*
> Identify and optimize your work cycles.

Common Work Cycles in Web Development

Let's look at common work cycles in web development. Figure 4.8 shows an overview of the four common work cycles in web development:

1. Real-time development work cycle (Edit-test work cycle)
2. Compare-update work cycle
3. Review work cycle
4. Major test work cycle

Real-Time Development Work Cycle

Many web developers and content contributors spend the bulk of their time using their preferred content creation tools, such as Photoshop, Dreamweaver, or Visual Studio. Figure 4.9 shows the web developer making edits in a work area copy of a complete set of web assets. Using the browser this developer invokes the modified assets on the web server, renders the modified assets, and views the results in his browser. That's the direct feedback paradigm in action. The rest of the real-time development work cycle is spent saving the changes and refreshing the browser. In contrast, a less effective work cycle without direct feedback might require the developer to FTP the files from his desktop machine to a web server before the changes could be viewed. This extra step slows down the cycle and reduces the developer's productivity. Indeed, even a minor interruption between the editing and the viewing

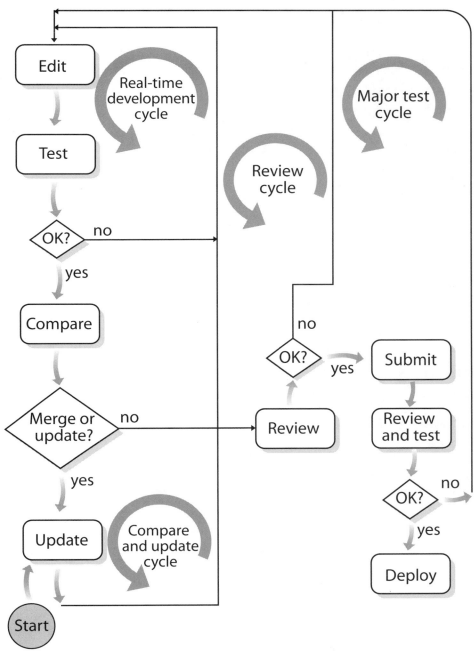

FIGURE 4.8
The four major work cycles in web development.

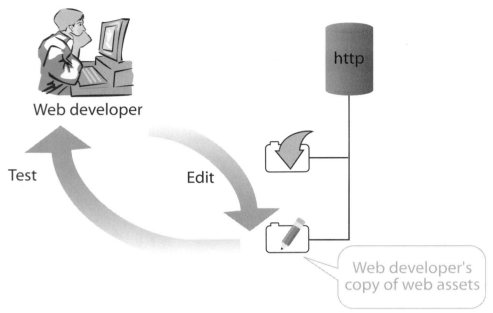

FIGURE 4.9
In the real-time development cycle a web developer edits and tests iteratively.

is enough to break the developer's train of thought. Evidence suggests that even minor interruptions in a content developer's work cycle introduce major productivity losses that are disproportionate to the actual delay.[2]

TABLE 4.3
A Best-Practice Web Development Process

Step	Description
1. Update	Get latest changes from staging area.
2. Edit	Make changes in work area.
3. Test	Test changes.
4. OK?	Do the changes work properly? If changes work, go to 5. Otherwise, go to 2.

---

[2]Mihaly Csikszentmihalyi, *Flow: The Psychology of Optimal Experience*, Harper Collins, 1991.

TABLE 4.3
A Best-Practice Web Development Process (Continued)

Step	Description
5. Compare	Compare work area against staging area.
6. Merge or update?	Are there changes in the staging area that need to be updated or merged into the work area? If yes, go to 7. Otherwise, go to 8.
7. Update	Get latest changes from staging area. Merge files if necessary. Go to 2.
8. Review	Reviewer inspects changes in work area.
9. OK?	Are the changes approved? If approved, go to 10. Otherwise, go to 2.
10. Submit	Submit changes to staging area.
11. Review & test	Review and test all changes in staging area.
12. OK?	Is the staging area a good web site? If staging area is good, go to 13. Otherwise, go to 1.
13. Deploy	Deploy changes to production.

Compare-Update Work Cycle

In the compare-update phase, a developer compares the assets in his work area to the corresponding assets in the staging area. The staging area contains updated assets that need to be periodically integrated into ongoing work, as other developers submit changes from other work areas. Figure 4.10 shows the compare-update work cycle.

Review Work Cycle

Figure 4.11 shows the review work cycle, which involves two kinds of specialists: a reviewer and a content developer. Although we'll describe the case of a single reviewer and a single developer, it is clear that this work cycle can be extended to more than one of each kind of specialist. A content developer completes their real-time development work cycle and present modified assets for review. For example, an artist asks an art director to review images, or proposed page layouts. A developer asks a peer to review changes made to programming source code. A template designer asks a business sponsor to review a common presentation template for all press release pages.

The reviewer checks the assets in the context of a functioning web site. This adheres to the direct feedback principle for the reviewer, and speeds the process. If the changes pass the review, the work cycle completes, and the assets are ready to be submitted to the staging area. If the assets aren't acceptable, then the developer edits and retests, and the assets are reviewed again.

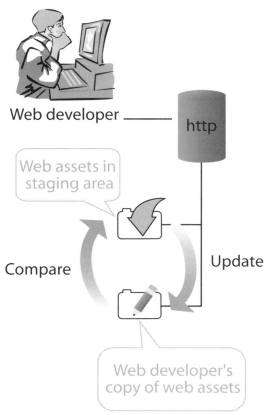

FIGURE 4.10
In the compare-update cycle a developer resolves differences between his work area and the staging area.

Major Test Work Cycle

Figure 4.12 shows the major test work cycle. A quality assurance (QA) engineer tests the assets in an edition. Following the direct-feedback principle, a web server renders the assets in the edition. If the testing proves successful, the edition is declared acceptable. If problems are discovered, defect reports are created and the respective developers are dispatched to resolve the problems. After review, changes are submitted to gather changes into the staging area. When appropriate, another edition is created and the major test work cycle continues. The need to cycle rapidly increases as a release deadline draws near. Just as separate work areas provide the ability for many developers to work in parallel, the major test work cycle accommodates many QA engineers working simultaneously.

Table 4.3 summarizes the steps in the four work cycles. The steps detail a best-practice development process.

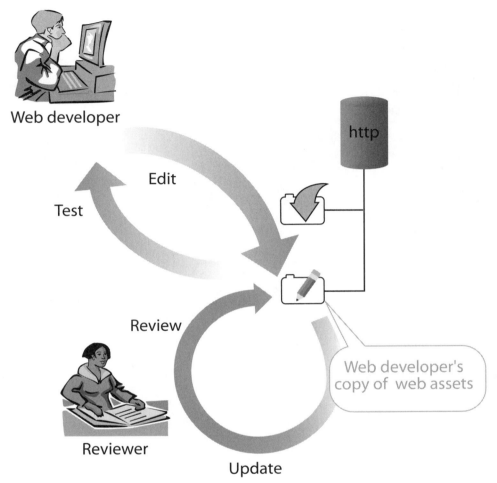

FIGURE 4.11
The review cycle identifies more edits to be made.

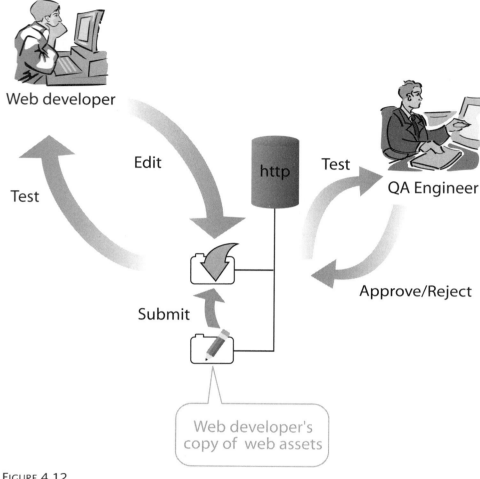

FIGURE 4.12
A QA engineer tests submitted content.

Summary

We've introduced the WSE paradigm, or the "work area/staging area/edition" paradigm. A work area is an area where a developer can work independently on a task. Completed, tested, and reviewed changes are submitted to a staging area, from which others can update their work areas, thereby staying synchronized with the group. An edition is a site-level version of a web property. A work cycle is a sequence of development steps related to creating, editing, testing, and reviewing assets. It often culminates in a feedback opportunity for a specialist, boosting efficiency and throughput. Typical work cycles in web development include the real-time development, compare-update, review, and major test cycles.

CHAPTER FIVE

TEMPLATING EMPOWERS CONTENT CONTRIBUTORS

Everything should be made as simple as possible, but not simpler.

—Albert Einstein

Executive Summary

Modern web sites are judged by what can be called the freshness directive, which mandates that a web site be constantly updated with fresh content. This imposes the following five requirements. First, a web site must have a design that is consistent overall. Second, a web site must evolve rapidly. Third, a web site must be continually updated with fresh content, with an economy of effort. Fourth, the web assets must be factored (separated out) to allow the web team to make changes concurrently. Fifth, a web site must have an efficient run-time architecture that lets it scale well under load. These requirements can be satisfied by a well-designed templating system. Reduced to its essence, a templating system separates content from presentation. We show an example of a templating system that satisfies these requirements.

77

Lost opportunity

In a 1920-era Midwestern brick office building converted to incubate several new economy dot-com's, Erin is a web producer for an advice web site, ePortal-Zone.com. Among other things, it offers free advice on selecting rollerblades. A freelance product tester had sent her a glowing first-person review of a hot new rollerblade from a local manufacturing firm. Erin could have posted the review last week if the look-and-feel revamp for the web site hadn't derailed her effort. The appearance redesign consumed all of this team's efforts to edit the existing content. Erin realizes that presenting a cool exterior look for ePortalZone.com is key to her company getting the next round of venture capital funding. However, she wonders if the inability to publicize a hot product from a local company is going to cause her to lose visitors to ePortalZone.com's web site.

As a die-hard rollerblade fanatic, Sam is eager to upgrade to a high-performance model. He clicks over to ePortalZone.com that a friend had mentioned. He checks the site regularly in his spare time at work, hoping for some advice on several new models that he had read about. But there is no news about rollerblades, and the last update was over a month ago. Disappointed, Sam clicks to a search engine to find a more up-to-date site.

Background

Many factors contribute to the success of a web site. Even though it is easy for a viewer to judge the outward appearance of a site, that viewer might be unaware that the internal structure of the site plays a vital role. Indeed, successful web sites by definition foster a multitude of repeat visits, and with all due respect to the designers of the visual appearance, after a number of visits, the importance of the overall look recedes and the ease of navigation and freshness factors start to take precedence. In this sense, a web site can be compared to a piece of physical architecture, like a home or a building. The outward appearance grabs our initial attention; we immediately notice the impressive sweep of the office building's entrance and façade, and the richness of the texture of the floors and walls. But, for a cubicle dweller who toils daily in the building, the novelty of the physical appearance fades, and practical concerns rise in importance. The robustness of the cooling system begins to matter greatly in the summer. The availability of usable meeting spaces and the degree to which the workspaces enhance or detract from productivity become far more important to the individual and to the organization over the long term.

The Freshness Imperative

Like a building, a web site has a visual presence and internal structural connections, and its interaction with a visitor evolves as the web site is used over time. Unlike a physical architectural artifact such as a building, however, a web site responds to a different set of expectations from its visitors. A visitor expects a web site to be simple to grasp, expressive in its intent, and comfortable to move about in. But there's more; we expect each visit to bring something new, and we have an unspoken desire for each visit to feel as if the entire web site were built a mere moment before we arrived. We refer to this as the *freshness imperative*. In this context, freshness could mean personalized content rendered for each specific visitor, or it could imply current content for everyone.

This explains why freshly cut flowers in a living or work space have such a strong psychological impact. By implication, a bouquet of blossoms in a vase of water speaks to us that it is there with us, sharing our space, brightening our experience, and by the way, it has been there for less than a few days.

In the same way, a "what's new" section of a web site adds a touch of freshness and aliveness that sets it apart from a web site devoid of change. This explains the psychological appeal of the "Last updated Wednesday, July 23" proclamation at the bottom of a web page; it tosses the viewer an assertion that, "Yes indeed, we've been actively updating this site. We mention this, because unless you look closely, you might not notice, and hence might not fully appreciate the effort we've put into this site." However, if a web site is actively updated, then it shouldn't be necessary to tell us that; instead, show us by our experience through the site.

The Challenge of Change

Building a modern web site poses many challenges. First, the site must look good, with a consistent overall design. Luckily, many web sites begin their life looking cool and compelling, especially with the plethora of web design shops offering their creative services. But the real challenge emerges in how well the web site stands the test of time. Will the once cool-looking site stay motionless, frozen in time, looking no different from the day that the creative shop FTP'd the assets a year ago? Will the in-house web team be able to take the design and use it to run a business? In other words, a web site must evolve and evolve rapidly—our second challenge.

For example, the perception of a good-looking site might be overturned overnight, when a tectonic shift such as a corporate merger renders a carefully tuned look-and-feel obsolete in one jolt. How fast a web site can be reconstructed with the redefined elements resulting from such a sudden event shows how well the site can handle the challenge of change.

Third, a web site must continually be updated with fresh content, with an economy of effort. Fresh material could be sale merchandise being promoted on a retail site, a "what's new" section on the homepage, or it could be as mundane as an updated site index page. Economy of effort means that it doesn't take an army of HTML coders to handcraft all of these changes, and the efficiency of effort means that updates can be undertaken more frequently. More frequent updates benefit web site visitors, while less required effort helps the web team by relieving stress, thereby making everyone more productive.

Fourth, the assets that comprise a web site must be factored in a way that allows many members of the web team to make changes concurrently. For instance, a content contributor might work concurrently with a creative services manager. A content contributor is someone whose domain of responsibility focuses on the information content within a web site. For example, a corporate communications manager might orchestrate a press release; her focus is the market positioning spin, the strategic sprinkling of third-party endorsements contained within the press release, and the go-live date of the release. At the same time, she doesn't need to be involved in the layout decisions of the press-release detail page, nor involved with the choice of font for the title on the press-release summary page. And she certainly has no desire to revisit all existing press releases to reformat them to the current design rules.

The same points can be made for the creative services manager charged with enforcing a consistent look and feel. He wants to have an HTML designer encode the revised look-and-feel design, for the press-release detail page, say, and then have the press-release pages regenerated all at once. There are too few hours in a day to hunt down every page to revise it, nor is there time to visually inspect every new hand-crafted press-release detail page.

Fifth, every web site needs an efficient run-time architecture that lets the web site perform well under load. In the pre-modern era of web sites, every page was static, and a web server basically served up the page efficiently, and did little else. The happy truth is that the pure static web sites performed remarkably well under load. But a web site consisting entirely of static pages imposed a monstrous burden on the developer to keep the content fresh. One of two things happened. Either a small army of HTML coders had to be hired to continually make changes, or the web site went stale. At best, the web site was updated less frequently than desired. There evolved a term for stale assets in a web site, "rot." Everyone quietly accepted that the web site that once looked fresh and compelling not so long ago, had begun to rot from the inside with outdated, incorrect, and inconsistent content.

The pendulum then began to swing in the other direction. In a sincere effort to make web site content fresher, web developers began to adopt application server technology. An application server replaced fixed coded HTML content with small programs, typically server-side Java code known as "servlets," to render content dynamically. With this quiet revolution, the concept of "dynamic content" suddenly came into vogue. It was a great relief that fresh content could be served, and web site rot could be slowed.

The negative side of this revolution has been the increased computational load imposed by the well-meaning use of application server technology. We all marvel at the way that the cost of computing hardware has fallen so predictably in our lifetimes. Yet at the same time, the greater reality is that adoption of web technologies and the rush of consumers and businesses alike to the Internet has outstripped the fall in the cost of server machines. As a result, web traffic to a successful web site almost always increases many times faster than the speed at which hardware costs decrease.

What's an example of overzealous use of dynamic web content? A simple example is the innocuous display of the current date. It takes only a line or so of code to render a string on a homepage, "Today is Thursday, June 20, 2002." For a highly visited web site this display is a problem. Let's take a moderately successful web site that has a million visits per day. Let's be generous and estimate that each invocation of the code to render the date string into HTML takes a mere millisecond. If we multiply by the visit count, the total is 1,000 seconds, or a quarter-hour of CPU time! This might seem small, but we've taken the smallest possible example, and it is big enough to be noticeable. Let's take a more visible example. Suppose a homepage, in its untiring effort to display up-to-date information, executes a database query to obtain the number of items marked for sale on a retail site, or the most frequently downloaded song on a music site. A database query is an expensive operation, perhaps ranging from 10 to 100 milliseconds each. On a million-visitor site, this represents somewhere between 2 and 30 hours of CPU time! If we look at it this way, it becomes obvious that a million-visitor-per-day site taking this approach faces a losing battle with scalability. After all, in our example, we inserted a single query on the homepage; there are likely to be many more queries of this kind elsewhere in a real web site.

The solution to this problem combines the best of dynamically rendered content, with the fast rendering of static content.

Enabling Change

Let's recap the challenges posed by the freshness imperative:

- A web site must have an overall design that is consistent.
- A web site must evolve rapidly.
- A web site must be continually updated with fresh content, with an economy of effort.
- The web assets must be factored to allow the web team to make changes concurrently.
- A web site must have an efficient run-time architecture that lets it scale well under load.

A Template System

Let's examine how a template system works, to see how it addresses these challenges. Figure 5.1 shows how information flows in a template system. We see that a content contributor is a source of data. A data-capture developer encodes the data entry and

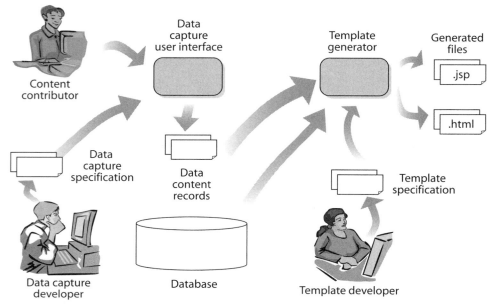

FIGURE 5.1

The content contributor, the data capture developer, and the template developer play different roles in the creation of the generated files.

validation logic that the data-capture user interface obeys. Another source of data is a relational database. The template developer creates a template specification asset, which encodes how to render the finished page, based on inputs from one or more data content records, and one or more databases. The generated files can be of many types. One example is a pure HTML page. It also could be a Java server page (.jsp), or a Java servlet.

Example: ezSuggestionBox.com

Let's illustrate how these concepts apply in an example. We consider a hypothetical company, ezSuggestionBox.com. It strives to be the industry-leader in the response processing industry. Its business is to produce co-branded portal sites that allow partner companies to collect, analyze, maintain, track, and respond to incoming suggestions from its customer base. A mock-up of a co-branded micro-site is shown in Figure 5.2. In this example, a partner company uses a template-generated web site specifically branded to render a suggestion portal. The General Bot Corporation builds automated software "robot" agents, sometimes referred to as a robot, or "bot" for short. One example of a bot might be automated software that scans, categorizes,

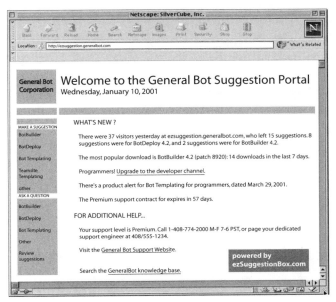

FIGURE 5.2
A template system generates a co-branded web site.

indexes, and prioritizes your incoming e-mail. In this example, General Bot uses a suggestion portal to solicit feedback from their community of developers.

In the same way, other customers have their own template-generated co-branded portal sites. This is shown in Figure 5.3. Notice that information on each page is customized for the particular customer.

Figure 5.4 shows where each section of the page derives its input. The customer-specific logo is referenced, based on which suggestion portal is being generated. The banner contains the date, which is rendered daily. Notice that because the date remains unchanged, it is only necessary to generate the banner once per day, instead of on each click. Interesting statistics are generated daily based on queries on the suggestion database. The support information is generated from customer and partner information contained in a database. This is rendered only when that information changes. The same is true about the contents of the navigation area; that are based on the licensed products, which are obtained by a database query. An application server generates the personalized feedback information about a specific person's suggestion status at click-time.

We see that all the content within the page that can be known in advance of click-time is pre-generated. In this example, this means everything except the user-specific

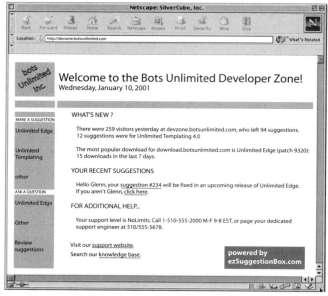

FIGURE 5.3
Another co-branded suggestion portal page displays personalized content in the "Your recent suggestions" section.

information. The site is efficient because the application server does the minimal amount of work possible to render a correct page.

Advantages of a Template System

Let's review the challenges that we posed earlier. In this example, the web site actually consists of the entire co-branded family of suggestion portal sites. Their overall design is dictated by a handful of template specification files. If a global change is required, then changing the one or two files, followed by a rebuild of all the templates will effect the change. For example, if the color scheme changes, the color constants are uttered in only a few places in the template specification files. If a more sophisticated scheme were needed, it could even be possible to obtain the color scheme files from a data content record, or from a database query.

This web site has carefully factored the elements that define its form and function. As a result, it can evolve quickly. For example, if ten new partners sign up in a single day, putting their co-branded sites into production consists of adding data content records, adding the associated database rows, and generating their portal pages.

This example shows that the need to be continually updated with an economy of effort is satisfied because nearly all of the content on the page is generated at template

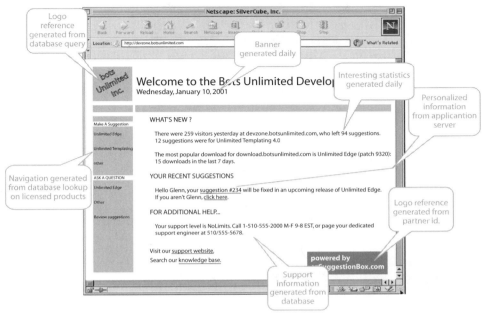

FIGURE 5.4
A generated page uses data from many sources.

generation time. Although there's an initial effort to specify the varieties of "interesting facts" sentences to generate, once that's done, the content regenerates daily.

The assets used in this example illustrate how content can be factored. The pure content relating to partner and customer information resides in data content records, or in a database. The visual look information is defined by various parameters in the template specification files. The logic specifying the automatically generated phrases are likely to be found in various program and script files that execute database queries on the suggestion to that point in time, and use that information to render into natural language various interesting facts. The important point is that because the content and logic are factored, they can be maintained, modified, and extended by different people concurrently. It would be much more difficult if all the presentation, database access, and rendering logic were all embedded into a single JSP or ASP asset.

It is interesting to notice that with some additional care, this system can easily be extended to support languages other than English. The language of choice to render the interesting facts will either be specified by the customer or by the specific user. For example, a user in the German subsidiary of General Bot Corporation (GBC) might choose to use the German-rendered suggestion portal page for GBC/Germany. Similarly, the personalized content would be rendered into German.

Finally, this example illustrates how the templating solution leads to an efficient run-time architecture. Specifically, nearly all of the queries, computation, and rendering have been moved to the template generation phase. Although an application server is used for personalization, the work has been partitioned to minimize the work left to the application server. The application server's work is on the critical path from the time the user's click is received, to the time that the browser can be sent the page contents. This has the simultaneous benefit that by making the handling of each click maximally efficient, the architecture scales well with increased load.

Summary

A well-designed templating system gives a web site a number of properties. It fosters a consistent visual design, an ability to be easily updated with fresh information, a factoring of the web assets to facilitate changes by many developers concurrently, and an efficient run-time architecture that lets the web site perform well under load.

Practitioner's Checklist

1. Collect samples of desired template output.
2. Identify content contributors and their inputs.
3. Tentatively define contents of data content record.
4. Create data capture form.
5. Create template specification; generate output.
6. Obtain client feedback. Iterate.

CHAPTER SIX

WORKFLOW SPEEDS WORK CYCLES

Never before have we had so little time in which to do so much.*

—Franklin Roosevelt

Executive Summary

Workflow is the process by which people collaborate to develop assets within a content management system. It applies to situations where multiple people collaborate on a job, where wait-time is a significant proportion of the total job time, and where patterns of interaction are repeated frequently. Workflow improves productivity by minimizing the wait-time between successive steps, and it automates the business logic of an organization. This chapter shows how to codify a pattern of interaction into a workflow job specification.

Using Workflow

Achieving a successful web site launch with the revamped look-and-feel requires precise teamwork. There can be no handoff delays, Dana thinks to herself. As web producer for the Olympics memorabilia auction site, Dana worked hard to hammer out a consensus for the look-and-feel for the entrance page. Competing agendas between the sponsors have delayed

continued

87

*Washington's Birthday Radio Address, February 23, 1942.

approval for two weeks. But now with the go-ahead firmly in hand, timing is critical. The launch of the sub-web site must coincide with television coverage of the opening ceremonies.

Luckily, the intense negotiations with the sponsors yields an electronic mock-up of the agreed-upon entrance page. Dana copies it into her work area and initiates a new workflow job. After filling the required fields in the job form, she attaches the mock-up. She recalls the bad old days, not long ago, when her mock-up consisted of a marked-up scrap of paper. The electronic mock-up will lead to fewer errors and less chance for confusion.

Dana feels anticipation as she starts the job because a carefully orchestrated chain of processes kicks in automatically. First, each web developer has an electronic to-do list, into which Dana's job immediately goes. Second, a pre-programmed script generates a notification to each web developer announcing the arrival of the job. Dana hopes that either Marielle or William will be able to accept the to-do item, but she hadn't seen either of them this morning in their cubicles or in their usual hangouts.

In the old days, Dana sent e-mails, made phone calls, left voice-mail messages, and attached sticky notes on chairs, in an effort to find someone who could handle a rush job. The company has grown so rapidly that merely finding a relocated person has become a chore. Here she is an experienced, highly paid web producer. Unfortunately, unproductive busy work consumes nearly all of Dana's time.

The new workflow-based scheme sports a custom notification subsystem that allows each developer to choose their preferred means of notification. Marielle stays with traditional e-mail, while William chooses to use an alpha pager because he spends so much time away from his desk.

William is working from home when he receives his pager notification. Because he had prior discussions with Dana about some of the design options, he is familiar with the choice that has been made. He connects to the workflow system to check his to-do list. He volunteers to accept Dana's assignment. By doing so, the workflow system removes the job from the to-do lists of the other developers.

William finds the work enjoyable. He finds it easier to concentrate while working at home, especially on jobs like Dana's memorabilia entrance page, because his mind finds a way to enter the ultra-productive state that performance psychologists like to call, "the flow." It feels to William like a few minutes, but when he emerges with the completed page, a full hour has passed. It is a productive hour, however, because he has completely redesigned the entrance page to follow the design direction laid out by the mock-up. He likes the result.

The next step in the pre-defined workflow specifies that another designer reviews his work. Dana's instructions in the job suggest two reviewers. William selects those two and adds a recently hired designer, Makenzie. William and Makenzie had collaborated on some recent projects. William appreciates Makenzie's pragmatic design sense.

William sends the job to the next step. That being done, William's attention shifts to his next job.

Behind the scenes, a scripted set of instructions stuffs the to-do list of the prospective reviewers and notifies them by their preferred means. Two of the reviewers are in all-day meetings, but the third, Makenzie, is at her desk. Upon receiving the notification, Makenzie pulls up the workflow user interface and clicks over to William's work. William has done a good job of implementing the look-and-feel, Makenzie thinks. She can see where William made some tricky color choices to accommodate the sponsors' logos without compromising the integrity of the page. She reviews Dana's design directives, and studies William's comments. She approves wholeheartedly, and expresses her enthusiasm in the job comments. Makenzie's approval pushes the job to the next step. The phone rings. Makenzie's focus shifts to the interruption.

Meanwhile, Dana sees Makenzie's approval confirmation e-mail after she returns from her morning staff meeting. It is barely eleven o'clock. The morning's activities exceed Dana's expectations for teamwork and efficiency. The ability to initiate a notification sequence, coupled with the ability to customize each developer's notification mechanism means minimal wait-time between steps. No more than a few minutes transpire between Dana starting the job, the development staff is notified, and the time when William volunteers to accept the job. Makenzie's review takes only a few minutes, but the true time saving arises from eliminating unnecessary waits for handoffs between people.

The workflow keeps the process orderly throughout. Its pre-configured business logic enforces the requirement for William's work to be reviewed by another designer before Dana is able to move the content into production. The notification subsystem speeds the handoffs between collaborators.

Characteristics of Web Development

Web development has characteristics that make it especially daunting for an organization to manage. The chemistry of web development brings together three key ingredients: a group of highly skilled people, a stream of incoming projects, and a business environment that rewards rapid execution and punishes mistakes. Understanding some of the workings of web development will help to clarify the role that workflow plays in improving productivity and in facilitating a smooth relationship among people, projects, and the business environment.

People Factors

Developing web assets involves many people with differing skills spanning many steps over an extended period of time. Web assets take many forms, touching our senses in varied ways: image, text, color, video, sound, layout, logic, linkage, and design. This multi-faceted nature of the assets introduces inescapable complexity into the development process. Producing a rich visitor experience on a web site requires a near-perfect blending of disparate skills. A project sponsor confers a blessing and provides resources. A marketing genius cooks up a scheme to attract a steady stream of visitors. A server-side Java developer encodes the logic behind a page. An artist designs the backdrop and design elements that inform the visual context. A writer selects words to evoke thoughts that guide us through the web visit. A lawyer keeps a legal watch for questionable material. A tester verifies that everything functions as a seamless experience. This blends the work of many contributors: a sponsor, a marketer, a developer, an artist, a writer, a lawyer, and a tester.

Many people contribute to the development effort. Contributors are physically separated, sometimes by multiple time zones. Skills vary widely, in terms of ability level and skill type. Distractions abound in the hectic world of web development. Consequently, tools must be easy to use. In particular, tools need to satisfy the needs of highly technical developers, as well as less technical folks that deal almost exclusively with web content, especially the "creative" folks: writers and artists.

Project Factors

A project forms the common framework in which a group of talented contributors collaborate to create the finished product. The goal might be relatively modest, such as repairing a misspelling in a corporate announcement on a high-traffic web page. It could be more ambitious, such as introducing an Olympics memorabilia section on an auction web site, combining the efforts of developers, artists, marketers, and business development hotshots.

A successful project fuses the team's accumulated knowledge into the machinery of the web. Through collaboration, the process of web development distills and refines the collective wisdom of the team into the web assets. When completed, the web assets run unattended on the production web site, ultimately embodying the creative knowledge and energy of the team.

The challenge for the development infrastructure is to make the collaboration run as smoothly and efficiently as possible. For instance, an asset is often sensitive to its context. Because of this, a project to modify or create context-sensitive assets needs to make sure that the developer can see the effect of their change in the appropriate context. For example, a graphic element is often placed on a page juxtaposed against another design element, such as another graphic. Let's suppose elements don't align properly. A specialist assigned to the task must be provided the context in which to make the change. For example, it isn't enough to merely attach the offending file into an e-mail message that says, "Hey you! The blue arc in this image needs to be nudged up and to the right, because it doesn't line up with the continuation of the arc in its adjoining image." Nor will it be enough to attach all the images to the e-mail, because the page into which the images are placed matters. Solving this kind of problem with an asset requires the appropriate context in which to make the fix. Solving this problem and also confirming that the fix has been done require viewing files in their proper context.

In this regard, web assets are similar to source code assets, where context has a strong influence. Just as a source code file uses the context defined by header files and just as it provides linkages for other code files, a graphic asset uses its enclosing page for placement information as it juxtaposes against other elements on the page. The challenge is to provide a way for many people to collaborate on many assets, in a tightly integrated manner. We'll see later how separate work areas provide for a collection of changes, and we'll see how this can be implemented within a workflow process.

Process Factors

Multiple people collaborate in multiple steps, and must do so as efficiently as possible. As with any multi-step job, the time can be divided into "think-time"[1] and "wait-time." It is *think-time* when the contributor does his or her part to advance the progress of the job as a whole. This is time spent in Photoshop™ altering the color and shape of a graphic element, or it is time spent reviewing a source code change. Sometimes, especially with multiple collaborators, think-time can be overlapped, so that the overall duration of the job can be reduced. In technical terms, there is a critical path, where the sum of the think-times along the critical path represents the shortest possible time in which the job can be completed. We'll define the *shortest-possible time* for a job, as the sum of the think-times along the critical path.

In many typical jobs, the actual time is often much longer than the shortest-possible time. We refer to the difference as *wait-time*. Consider the example from the introduction. The structure of the job is simple: a task for a developer to create new web assets, followed by a task for a reviewer to approve or not approve the changes, followed by a task to present the approved work to the originator. A delay anywhere along the chain delays the completion of the job by a like amount.

Web development is a people-intensive activity. Although computers obviously play an important role, people are almost always the scarce resource and the gating factor

---

[1] The concept of "think-time" and "wait-time" appears in http://www.oreview.com/9802hari.htm, http://www.microsoft.com/technet/win2000/win2ksrv/technote/perftune.asp, http://www.hp.com/pressrel/sep99/07sep99b.htm, and http://www.ed.gov/databases/ERIC_Digests/ed370885.html.

for success. Notification minimizes wait-times by making a person aware of an incoming task as soon as it is ready. Factories in early nineteenth-century America drove down production costs by improved efficiency through the use of the factory assembly line, combined with related innovations of interchangeable parts, and skill specialization. In the same way, a workflow and its interrelated tasks act like a virtual assembly line.

The work products "flow" from person to person, as defined by the workflow definition. Just as an assembly line in a factory physically arranges the flow of partially assembled goods to move past people at workstations, a workflow moves web assets through various stages of completion and approval through a pre-defined set of steps. Like physical locations on a factory floor, the workflow steps relate to the requirements of the procedural flow as codified in the workflow definition. These correspond to checkpoints required by the business and organizational environment. For example, Dana's workflow embodies a distinct step where the web developer's work is reviewed and explicitly approved. This is analogous to an inspection station in a physical assembly line.

Web development differs in one important respect from physical manufacturing processes. There is an overlapping mixture of quick-turnaround and long-term projects, which means that a given person may be involved in several projects at the same time. Different people participate in each project, and it becomes impractical to arrange people contributing to successive steps to be physically adjacent. In comparison, the assembly line boosts efficiency by arranging manufacturing steps into close physical proximity. Despite physical separation, the workflow binds the participants together.

Business Factors

The rate at which assets change to keep up with the pace of business continues to accelerate. Even as the different skills come together to create more elaborate web properties, the speed at which people and organizations are expected to move continues to increase. In part, competition drives the pace. If technology allows a company to move quickly, then the company will do so, or their competition will pull ahead.

A workflow reinforces an organization's ability to codify its key business processes. A workflow adds a process infrastructure to assist the members of the organization to assure that key steps in the process are followed. For example, a workflow assures that all content deployed to the production site has been formally reviewed and approved by a quality assurance team.

Virtual Assembly Line

A workflow system addresses the difficulties that accompany web development. It acts as a *virtual assembly line* in which the three key factors of web development interact: people, projects, and a business environment. On this virtual assembly line, people work on the tasks that compose a project. A project needs to be moved from one task to another, with minimal delay between tasks. The new and modified assets for a project are held in a work area where all the contributors can see, test, review, and approve their changes in the context of a functioning web site. The business environment needs review, approval, and other established process steps to be followed. It seeks to maximize project throughput while using resources efficiently.

Consider the example shown in Figure 6.1. Three people, in three different departments, collaborate on a typical small job. A producer in the marketing department determines that a part of the web site needs to be changed. The producer initiates a job, hands off the job, requesting design assistance from the graphic arts department. A designer is assigned to the job, and proceeds to fulfill the request. When the designer is complete, she hands it off to a reviewer in the quality assurance department. After the reviewer signs off on the work, the job returns to the producer.

 Figure 6.2 shows these steps along a timeline. At the point where the producer hands the job off to the designer, the designer may be busy on another job. Eventually, the designer becomes available, and commences her part of the job. She hands off the work.

There are three kinds of time: think-time, busy-wait time, and idle time. Think time is useful time spent on the job, as described earlier. The rest is wait-time, of which

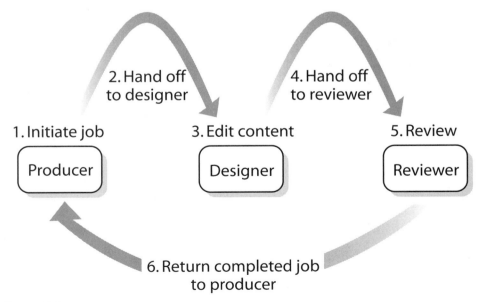

FIGURE 6.1
A simple three-step job has three hand-offs.

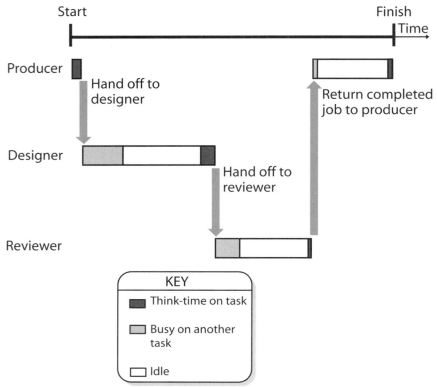

FIGURE 6.2
The time for a job consists of busy-wait-time, idle-time, and work-time.

there are two kinds. Busy-wait time means that the recipient of the job is busy completing other jobs. Idle time means the recipient is able to take another job, but work on the job has not started. *Busy-wait time* is unavoidable, because other useful work occupies the recipient of the next task. *Idle time* is waste, never to be reclaimed. In a physical assembly line, close physical proximity of work stations eliminates idle time. In a virtual assembly line, notification eliminates unnecessary idle time. Figure 6.3 illustrates this point.

The virtual assembly line overcomes the difficulties introduced by multiple contributors who need to work closely in a short period of time. To produce the richness of experience that everyone has come to expect from the web requires orchestrating the contributions of many collaborators. The effort needs to be tightly coordinated. A virtual assembly line built using a workflow solution orchestrates the activities of the transient group to complete assigned tasks quickly and efficiently.

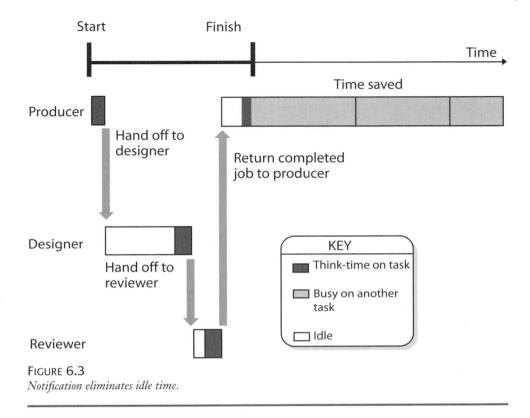

FIGURE 6.3
Notification eliminates idle time.

To summarize, a workflow solution enables the timely development of web assets. Many different people, with widely varying skills, contribute to the web development effort. Although there are multiple overlapping projects, each project needs to be handled on a virtual assembly line. Each project creates and modifies assets that may change the context of other assets. Because of frequent change and tight deadlines, maintaining a rapid pace of development is essential. An infrastructure to notify participants upon completion of intermediate tasks boosts productivity by minimizing costly idle time. Finally, by codifying processes and procedures, a workflow improves the consistency and efficiency of the organization's actions.

Workflow Concepts

Now that we've seen some of the benefits of a workflow solution, let's look at the concepts behind designing and building a workflow.

Interaction Pattern

The basic premise behind the workflow paradigm is that the process of developing web assets consists of frequently repeated interaction patterns between people, projects, and the business. For example, it is very typical for a web development group to need a way to track small or medium-sized changes to a web site. For instance, someone discovers a misspelling in a block of text, a contact address changes, an outside party objects to the appearance of an image, or HTML code is found to be incompatible with a particular version of a browser.

On the surface, each such change is simple to handle. The change itself requires a simple edit to a graphic, or to a text file. Getting it reviewed and approved takes only a minute or so. Moving the change into production entails copying a handful of files. But the volume and frequency of the changes means that the process is far from simple. Difficulty comes from the interaction from juggling many changes simultaneously. As contributors juggle more projects, the coordination overhead increases. Idle time on a project outweighs the work time, dragging down throughput.

One key to success is to isolate each change into a work area, to minimize the interactions between changes when the individual edits are done, and to facilitate testing. A work area provides the context in which the changes will be made. In the virtual assembly line, the work area is the work cell that circulates among the collaborators. Joining in at the appropriate time, each participant in a virtual assembly line sees the work of the others.

The next step is to identify a frequently repeated pattern of interaction between developers. The exact people might vary, and the precise assets involved might vary, but you should look for a pattern of repeated interaction. For instance, a web producer assigns work to the development group, someone in the group volunteers to take the assignment, the developer hands off the work to a reviewer, and the reviewer hands it back to the producer. That is a pattern. Focus on the task that each person performs, and the handoff to the next person. After a pattern is identified, represent the interaction as a related set of tasks.

Tasks

A task represents an activity. Table 6.1 shows the possible kinds of tasks.

Job

Our goal is to define a workflow job specification, which codifies the sequencing and dependencies of the interactions as a collection of workflow tasks. A *workflow job specification* is a program that creates an instance of a workflow job. We call an instance of a workflow job specification a *job*. The workflow job specification program usually presents a user interface with which to solicit additional details about the job. For example, when Dana creates a workflow job for her Olympics memorabilia page, the

TABLE 6.1
A Workflow Job is Composed of Tasks.

Kind of Task	Description	Workflow Task
Individual assignment	Assign user a to-do item.	User task
Group assignment	Propose a to-do item to a group of people; one member of the group may volunteer to take the assignment.	Group task
User interaction	Interact with user via a browser (display information, accept information, or take some action on behalf of the person).	CGI task
External	Execute a scripted action on behalf of the user.	External task
Submit	Submit files from a work area into the staging area.	Submitt task
Update	Update a work area with latest changes from staging area, or copy assets from one work area to another.	Update task
End	End the job.	End task

program asks her for a description of the tasks, the group that should receive the assignment, the person who should review the work, deadlines for the project, and other pertinent details. The program may also access a database or a configuration file for permissions or e-mail addresses. The program uses these inputs to specify the tasks that constitute this instance of the workflow.

Transition Links

A job consists of tasks that are connected to one another by *transition links*. Transition links define how the completion of one task activates one or more successor tasks, and appear as the arrows between the task boxes in Figure 6.4.

Active and Inactive Tasks

A task is either active or inactive. When a job is created, all of its tasks are inactive, except for one or more designated *start tasks*. The state of a workflow is determined by the active tasks. For example, if a user task is active, that means that the job waits for the assigned person to perform the desired task. When an active task completes, a transition occurs to another task, which then becomes active. If there is exactly one transition link to another task, then the transition is unconditional. If there are two or more transition links, then the user or some other conditional logic chooses which other task or tasks to transition to.

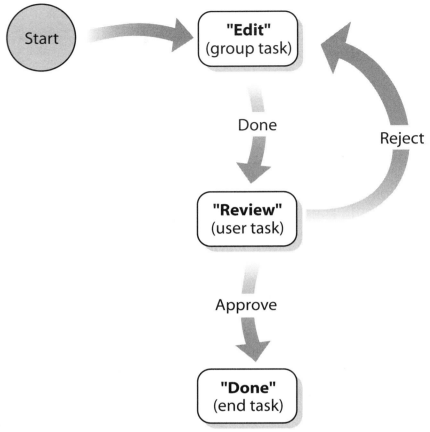

FIGURE 6.4
A simple arrangement of tasks for a workflow.

Building a Workflow

Let's describe how to codify the pattern of interaction into a workflow. Figure 6.4 shows a simple arrangement of tasks for a bare-bones workflow. There are three tasks. The job starts at a group task, which we refer to as "Edit." A group task allows anyone in a certain group to volunteer to complete the task. After editing by that person is complete, the task unconditionally transitions to a user task, which we've named, "Review." If the reviewer chooses the "Approve" transition, the link takes the job to the "Done" task, which completes the job. If the reviewer chooses the "Reject" transition, the state goes back to the "Edit" task.

This example shows how a job can be composed of different kinds of tasks, and the different roles that the task types play. For example, the group task allows any member of a group to volunteer to take ownership of a task. This example also shows how some situations use an unconditional transition to a next task, and it shows where it makes sense to have a choice of transitions. The review task that has a choice of "Approve" or "Reject" is an example of a conditional transition.

When a job is created, the tasks, and relationships between tasks are specified. Details include such things as who is assigned the task, which task precedes another, or which files are being modified. Some aspects of the job are fixed at the time the workflow is instantiated, but others can be changed after instantiation. For example, is the reviewer assigned to the "Review" task known when the job is instantiated? For some organizations, the answer is yes because there is one designated reviewer for all work done by a given group. For another organization, the answer is no because the reviewer isn't known in advance. Perhaps the person doing the "Edit" task is best suited to choose the reviewer. There is no unequivocal right or wrong answer; the choice is best made by the organization. To the workflow designer, this question is important because it affects the design of the workflow job specification.

Notification

Figure 6.5 shows the same workflow augmented with external tasks to implement notification of relevant personnel. Recall that when many people are involved, it is important to minimize wait-time when work is handed off from one person to another. Whether notification is implemented by e-mail, pager, or other scheme, the effect is to make sure that the job proceeds as if on a virtual assembly line. A physical assembly line in a manufacturing facility uses the arrival of a partially completed unit to notify the worker at the next assembly station. In contrast, notification plays a critical role in a virtual assembly line precisely because successive steps are usually separated.

Designing a Workflow

This section sketches a roadmap for designing a workflow job specification.

1. Identify Interaction Sequences

Start the design process by identifying the areas that would benefit from having a workflow job specification built for it. Look for repeated, frequent interaction sequences between people and projects. The business environment will be characterized by multiple people, tight deadlines, intolerance for delays due to people waiting on each other, and high need for precise adherence to established processes. Identify a handful of patterns to investigate more fully. Make an estimate of the benefits to the organization. Benefits are likely to be gained in terms of the following:

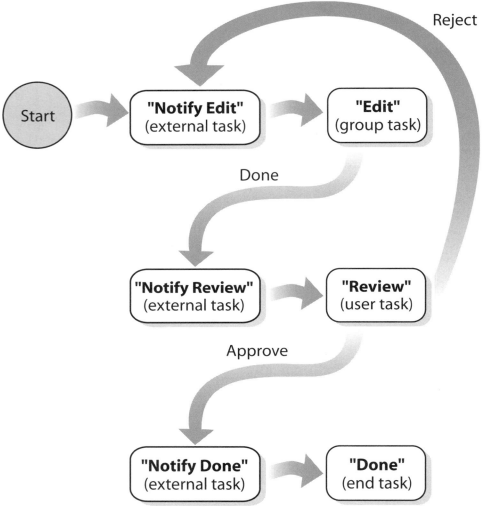

FIGURE 6.5
A workflow augmented with external tasks provides notification.

1. Making the process more efficient by saving in people time
2. Eliminating waiting time by having more effective hand off steps
3. Reducing chance of errors because of more formal handling of tasks
4. Adhering better adherence to processes and standards
5. Undertaking more ambitious web initiatives

Focus on frequently repeated interaction sequences, because the benefit is proportional to the benefit accrued per task, times the number of times that the sequence occurs.

2. Identify Candidate Workflow

Identify a Logical Point for the Job to Start

With a handful of candidate interaction sequences identified, and with a rough sense of the benefit payback to the organization, represent the flow in terms of the basic task types described earlier. Ascertain when a job starts, and when the job ends. Usually a job starts on some incoming event. For example, a marketing manager initiates a change request to the web site, or an automated content feed has arrived which needs to be processed with a combination of automatic and manual steps.

Identify a Logical Point to End the Job

End a job at the point where the incoming event has been satisfactorily handled. In addition, the point at which activity quiets down marks the completion of a job. For example, a job that starts on an incoming request to make a change to a web site may be deemed to be complete when the requested changes have been deployed to the web site. Alternatively, the request may be considered handled when it has been prioritized and batched for further handling by a developer. In this latter case, a follow-on workflow can be generated that combines one or more incoming requests. This example shows that there is latitude for choosing job boundaries to best fit the typical usage situation.

3. Sketch the Steps

With the start and finish of a job tentatively known, proceed to block out the tasks required to implement the job. On the first few design iterations, omit the notification steps. By temporarily ignoring the notification steps you're able to more clearly highlight the flow of the work. Add the notification later.

Step through the normal path of the job. In other words, suppose that all reviews lead to approval, and no error situations are encountered. This is the time to hone in on what really constitutes desired handling of the job. Are there multiple contributors? If yes, can they operate in parallel, or must they be one after the other? Are there reviewers or approvers? At this point you'll probably want to engage in further discussions with the users of the workflow system to validate how well the skeleton workflow layout represents the variety of situations that it will be used in. Check with the sponsors of the effort to ascertain whether key business requirements are captured in the workflow. Is an explicit approval required on every change? Who is authorized to give approval?

Check for Potential Bottlenecks

Someone may claim that a specific person should personally sign off on every change, but the person expressing this sentiment may not literally mean this restriction. Find out if the approval can be made by a wider set of people. Perhaps, too, it might be sufficient for a core set of people to be made aware of every change, instead of some one person being a choke point in the process. Suggest alternatives. Perhaps it is adequate for e-mail to be generated to keep key people apprised, instead of requiring formal approval.

Beware of Long Task Chains

When engaging in design discussions with the prospective users of the workflow, you sometimes hear an expansive list of contribute and review steps, all of which apparently need to be encoded into a long chain of tasks within the job specification. If you build a workflow specification based literally on this requirement, a long task chain emerges in the workflow.

Example—Simplifying a Workflow

Let's look at an example of workflow simplification. A business manager might initiate a job, then passes the task to a web producer, who assigns it to a web developer. After the web developer completes the task, she passes it to a manager for review, who passes it to the quality assurance manager, who assigns it to a quality assurance engineer, who passes it back the originating business manager. Superficially, this long list of contributors sounds appealing in concept, because it guarantees that everything produced by such a process will be checked, and rechecked. But you need to separate the intent of the design from the actual implementation. In the example here, the intent is clearly for each job to pass through enough checking to maintain high quality. Let's explore various ways to simplify this workflow, while being faithful to the underlying intent.

The proposal described above consists of the following steps:

1. Business manager initiates.
2. Web producer assigns.
3. Web developer creates and edits.
4. Manager reviews.
5. QA manager assigns.
6. QA engineer tests and verifies.
7. Business manager confirms.

Start with the business manager. Ask about the current mechanism by which a business manager conveys a project to web producers. In a typical organization, business needs are identified, and these translate to specific web projects. The project scope probably emerges from a face-to-face discussion between a business manager and a web producer. If this is the case, then it probably makes more sense to have the web producer initiate the workflow job, instead of the business manager.[2] If we take this approach, we can arrange for the job to notify the business manager by e-mail that the job has commenced. We see that the business manager initiates the job, but the workflow itself doesn't reflect this, nor does it need to. After all, computers don't have to know everything!

With this revision, the web producer initiates a job. Web producers will be doing this frequently, based on verbal requests from the business folks. In the original proposal, the job is assigned to a web developer. Alternatively, we can allow any web developer to volunteer for the job. To implement the former, we use a "user task," while the latter uses a "group task." At this early juncture, we don't need to precisely nail down which paradigm to use. We can pick one and proceed with the rest of the design.

Let's suppose that in this example, that there is a heavy volume of jobs flowing from web producer to web developer. It makes sense to use the workflow system to represent the assignment as a formal step in the job specification. The job has transitioned to the web developer.

At this point, a decision arises that is commonly faced when designing a workflow. There might be multiple developers assisting on the job. For example, the web producer might assign the job to a lead developer, who in turn enlists the help of other developers. Perhaps an editor specializes in writing prose, while an artist focuses on graphic elements. One option is to allow the lead web developer to invoke another task to formally convey the assignment to one or more contributors. This approach works if there is a heavy volume of jobs, and the jobs are rigidly structured to lend them to a predetermined task sequence. The think-time is relatively small compared to the typical wait-time, and helpers don't always work in close vicinity of one another. In other words, formal workflow support in passing tasks during the editing phase helps to keep the project overhead from overwhelming the project think-time.

A second option is to let the lead developer orchestrate the activities of the helpers within the designated work area. The assets to edit reside in a designated work area, and helpers are called in as needed to complete the work. This approach works if jobs vary widely in the task sequence, and helpers work in close proximity. Varying widely in task sequence means that some jobs are simple, say, requiring one HTML editor, while some require multiple HTML specialists, Java coders, and graphic artists. In the second, more informal approach, the work of many people is represented in the workflow as a single task.

---

[2] This has the additional benefit of eliminating the need to train the business managers about using a new tool!

Continuing our example, the original proposal specifies management approval after the web developers complete their work. Now we need to ask what we mean by "approval." To give this concrete meaning, let's say that 100 jobs per week pass through the workflow system. On one hand, approval could mean that a team of approvers explicitly approves 100 jobs weekly. On the other hand, the same business need to "approve" might be met if recently completed jobs were available for informal review by the approvers. The latter scheme allows the flexibility for the high-visibility or high-risk jobs to be scrutinized carefully, while avoiding the need for formal go-ahead on each change.

A better approach is to delegate formal approval of content to the quality assurance staff. They will be more likely to have the capacity to handle the job flow. For example, a relatively small QA staff ought to be equipped to pass formal judgment on 100 jobs per week. In addition, if others need to be kept in the loop, both managers and interested stakeholders, this can be accommodated through notification at critical junctures.

We've streamlined the job flow, and introduced an alternate simpler design. We obtain the more compact scheme shown below:

1. Web producer (initiator) (Business manager notified at job creation.)
2. Web developer (Manager notified when task is completed.)
3. QA engineer (QA manager notified when task completed.)
4. Web producer (Multiple notifications when last task completes.)

Many of the steps that we envisioned in the original proposal as discrete steps have been replaced by notification, or by direct face-to-face interaction. The fundamental intent of the workflow has been retained.

Iterate Your Design

Allocate a block of time to investigate design alternatives, and avoid the temptation to endlessly design and redesign. When you've exhausted the allotted time to explore alternatives, commence with a prototype. Keep in mind that people's perceptions of the system will change and evolve as it is used, so be flexible about all suggestions and requirements. If you are unsure about going with something simpler or something else less simple, go with the simpler approach. You'll be able to get it working sooner, and thereby get valuable feedback more quickly. If your approach turns out to be vastly different from what people really want, a simpler design is easier to discard or rewrite.

4. Identify Known and Not-Yet-Known Parameters

One of the tricky parts about writing a workflow job specification is proper handling of parameters that aren't known when the job is created. For example, if the reviewer of a set of changes is known at the time the job is created, then other aspects of the design fall into place simply. For example, the owner of the work area can be encoded, as well as the work area itself.[3]

Even though some information is not known at job creation time, you can be assured that the information will become known at some point during the life of the job. Will it be gathered during a browser interaction with one of the users? Will it be obtained during script processing? If yes, then make provision for either adding an explicit CGI-task step to gather the information, or determine how that information will flow from the point it is determined, to where it will be used.

5. Add Remaining Transitions

When the normal case of the workflow fits the requirements of your situation, proceed to add the transitions for the rest of the cases. Examine each step of the job. Identify all tasks that can provide information that alters the flow of the job from the normal path. What happens if an approver rejects the work? What if an external script coded to do spell-checking finds errors? What if the submit step encounters conflicts that need to be resolved?

Allocate time to think through the "not approved," "redo," and "reject" transition paths. A good rule of thumb is to allocate an equal amount of time for this phase of the design as the earlier "Sketch the steps" phase. This makes sense when you realize that for every path to make forward progress within a workflow job there will likely be two, three, or four ways for the job to move backward. This reinforces the idea of keeping the initial design simple: a simpler design for forward progress will tend to make the model for backward movement simpler too. To emphasize the importance of thinking through the backward paths, make a list of all the tasks that have backward transitions, and record who initiates such a transition, what their intended meaning is, and what the job state becomes after the transition. The list of backward paths will be useful in the testing phase. Finally, don't be surprised if you decide to remove some steps entirely based on your analysis of the backward transitions; this is good, because you'll have a workflow that is simpler to understand, simpler to implement, simpler to explain, and simpler to test.

6. Add Notification Steps

Add the notification steps last. Why? First, since notification sends information out of the job, it cannot alter the flow of the job, and hence it doesn't impact the design. That's why we're able to add it in at the end of the design phase. Second, you'll discover precisely how many notification points your design uses at the end of the design

---

[3] If the reviewer is not or cannot be known in advance, a technique such as the one described in Appendix B that supports formal handoff between groups can be used.

phase. Knowing how many notification points and taking stock of what kind of message each notification point will be obligated to send will itself give you valuable insight into how to approach implementation. The notification points will reveal specific requirements about what the e-mail messages need to contain. Keep in mind that the users of the system will spend a significant portion of their time reading the e-mail messages that notify them of task transitions. The e-mail text represents a significant portion of the interface that the system presents to users.

Notification can also be used to remind assignees of pending tasks that have not been completed within a certain amount of time. This is done using a "timeout" specification for the specific task, which can transition to the reminder notification task and then back to the original task.

Summary

Web development encompasses creation, modification, review, and approval of assets for eventual use in a web site. Web development has characteristics that make it exceedingly difficult for an organization to manage. These characteristics encompass people, project, and business factors.

The key to overcoming these difficulties is to use a workflow infrastructure to combine people, projects, and a business environment into a virtual assembly line. In a virtual assembly line, a highly skilled contributor is presented with a task to perform, in the context of other related assets, where the required task can be completed efficiently. Upon completion of the task, the contributor transitions the job to the next task and to the next contributor with minimal delay. This works harmoniously with the business environment, because all of this occurs within established processes and procedures. Errors and process failures are minimized.

A number of concepts underpin the workflow paradigm. An important foundation is the identification of repeated patterns of interaction between people, projects, and the business environment. The patterns are codified into workflow job specifications, which are programs that run within the workflow infrastructure to create workflow jobs. A workflow job consists of tasks that are related by transition links.

A good workflow design consists of a structure that meets requirements: as simple as possible, but no simpler. The goal is to identify interaction sequences for which codifying into workflow jobs will reap benefits to the organization. Benefits include the following:

- Saving time
- Increasing throughput by eliminating waiting
- Reducing errors
- Improving adherence to established processes
- Allowing greater ability to undertake web initiatives

Practitioner's Checklist

1. Identify interaction sequences.
2. Identify candidate workflow for more detailed investigation.
3. Sketch the steps.
4. Identify known and not-yet-known parameters.
5. Add remaining transitions, especially "backward transitions."
6. Add notification steps.

CHAPTER SEVEN

DEPLOYING CONTENT

For time is the longest distance

between two places.   —*Tennessee Williams*

Executive Summary

Deployment comprises the processes and practices by which web assets that have been reviewed and approved are copied from a development environment to a production environment. Web assets include files, directories, and database elements. The goal of a deployment infrastructure is to copy assets to the production server into the right location at the appropriate time. Assets no longer on the development side are deleted from the production side. An important organizational underpinning of a deployment infrastructure is the release agreement, which binds the development and production groups into a social contract. Content and application developers agree to approve and formally submit any asset to be deployed, and production server administrators agree to use only released assets on a production server. In a well-designed deployment infrastructure, only someone that is authorized to initiate a deployment job does so. There is confirmation of success or a notification of failure so that remedial action can be taken. The primary benefit of this arrangement is that asset changes are copied into production with minimal or no effort, with full control, notification, and the ability to roll back to a known-good version.

109

Introduction

"What's wrong with the product information subsystem on our external site?" Valerie asks David. Her soft-spoken voice carries an insistence that David dares not dismiss. It is 10:15 A.M. on Thursday, and the corporation's worldwide online store web site is broken. As a web producer, Valerie discovered the problem while checking a product promotion that she intended to change. Her tests reveal that the store locator section of the web site isn't functioning. She decides to inform David.

Quickly, David grasps the mouse of his workstation, and his shortcut brings up the homepage. Eyes focus on David's browser, where an error screen pops unceremoniously onto David's screen:

"Permission denied. The URL cannot be accessed," the dialog box declares coldly.

Valerie saw exactly the same problem moments ago. Silence fills David's cubicle. Each person's mind traces the many steps ahead. Thousands of potential customers per minute hit the web site at this time of day; and perhaps half of them will encounter the error screen.

Rectifying the problem will take many laborious steps and require coordination with several other groups within the corporation. The web development group and the web operations group will need to back out recent code changes to the product information section of the web site. They'll have to find Linnea, who manages that group, and hope that she can track down the developer who made the changes. If everything goes well and everyone cooperates, this will take a few hours. Since this is the middle of a weekday, the count of improperly handled web hits might reach into the tens of thousands. That would be a painful blow to the company's early efforts to build a web presence.

David's neurons race more quickly than most people's do. In his previous job, he administered a web site for a local video store, and he immediately grasps the magnitude of the problem. While Valerie envisions the disappointed web visitors, David determines that the content management system had already captured a full snapshot of the external web site. Luckily, this occurred before the recent changes that were possibly the cause of the problem.

David opens the content management interface, selects a known-good edition, and instructs the system to roll back to the known-good web site. In less than a minute the external web site is restored to the prior state. Everything works again.

Concept Review

Deployment is the process of moving web assets onto one or more production servers. Most web operations do deployment, which has the important effect of separating the process of developing, testing, and approving a web site, which we call *development*, from the serving of the resulting web assets, which we call *production*. Deployment divides the creative but sometimes messy job of creating and testing the web site, from the serving of those assets to the outside world, including the corporate Intranet, the public at large, and partners organizations on an extranet. Figure 7.1 shows how deployment copies web assets from development to production.

Although this is conceptually simple, there are many details to attend to. The major decisions have to do with configuration: allowing authorized people to deploy, denying access to unauthorized people, and agreeing on kinds of deployment (immediate, scheduled) to implement. The stakeholders are the groups that are responsible for the content, for the production server(s), for the network, and for security.

Recall from Chapter 3 that development consists of the creation, testing, and approval of content, text, graphics, and programming logic. The job of development is to combine editorial, creative, and programming inputs to produce a released version of a web site. This is shown in Figure 7.2. Recall that a released version of a web site is the complete set of web assets corresponding to a given point in time. We'll also refer to the released version as simply a *version* of a web site. We use the term web asset in a broad sense; a *web asset* is a file, a directory, or a row in a database table.

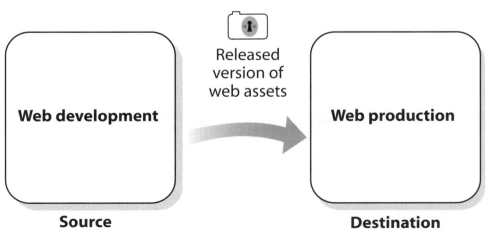

FIGURE 7.1
Deployment moves developed web assets to one or more production servers.

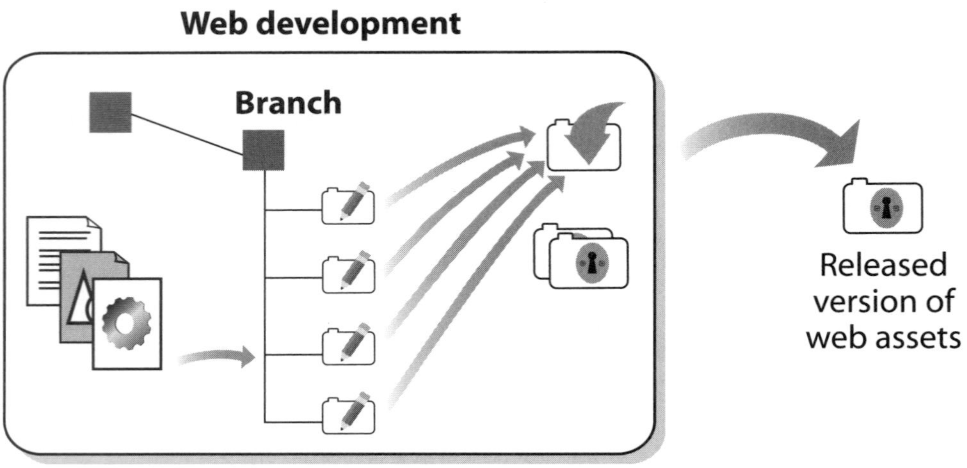

Web development

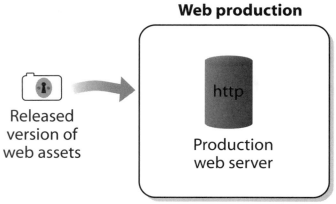

FIGURE 7.2
A released version of the web assets is an important deliverable from the development process.

Web production consists of the rendering of the released version of web assets on one or more servers, possibly geographically dispersed, for use by the target audience of the web site. The job of production is to accept the released version of a web site and to serve the content to the target audience. This is shown in Figure 7.3

Web production

FIGURE 7.3
The production process serves the released version of the web assets to the target audience.

The Release Agreement

The fundamental job of deployment is to copy a version of web assets from development to production. There is an important assumption underlying this simple model, which we refer to as the release agreement. According to the *release agreement*, the development group agrees to designate a tested and approved version of the web site, and the production group agrees to serve that content on production servers.

On the development side of the release agreement, the released version is known to be correct and complete, in terms of content and functionality. For example, on a corporate portal web site, the press releases are timely and accurate, and the links to other parts of the site work as advertised.

The release agreement focuses each member of the development team on the goal of creating the released version as efficiently as possible. Essential to smooth operation of a large team, it serves as an empowering force for web specialists on the development team. For example, suppose you work on the development side. You continually ask yourself, "How close is our team to completing the released version of our web site, and what is going to be my contribution to that release?" If you are an artist, you want to know whether all the visual elements on the site are complete, and what the result looks like. When working with other members of the development team, you ask, "How does my effort integrate with the work of others, and how close are our combined efforts to a released version?" If you are a graphic designer, you want to know whether your visual design complements the navigational logic implemented by the Java developers.

On the production side of the release agreement, the production group agrees to deploy the released version of the web site to one or more production servers—no more and no less. The release agreement says that the production process transparently moves assets from development to the various production servers.

The release agreement simplifies the task of tracking down problems. In the real world, problems and breakdowns inevitably occur. The ability to isolate and identify the cause of a problem quickly is essential. Let's consider an example. Suppose that there are sporadic reports of problems in the press-release area; in particular, certain press releases appear to be missing. Since there is a released version of the web site to refer to, it is possible to isolate the problem by examining the released version. Are the missing press releases there? If yes, then the problem is probably somewhere in the production process or procedures. For example, did all the deployment scripts run to completion without errors? Did the deployments to the multiple production servers run successfully? If a production web server needs to be cycled down and up on a deployment, did that procedure function correctly? We see that questions like these help to isolate the cause of the faulty web pages on the production side.

Similarly, if the press releases are missing in the released version, then the breakdown lies in the development side. To isolate the problem on the development side, we ask additional questions. Was the press release submitted? Was it reviewed and approved? Was it overwritten by another change? Was it released, and then later retracted?

The steps involved in locating a problem underscore the importance of building an infrastructure that is maintainable, repeatable, and reliable. A good deployment infrastructure does more than merely deploying files. It provides a framework for finding the underlying problem quickly and efficiently when something goes wrong. In our example, we see that it can be a challenge just to determine whether the problem resides on the development side or on the production side. Having a known reference point of the released version is an important starting point. Once that is determined, there are many additional points of investigation. You want to be able to identify the problem with a minimum of diagnostic steps.

To summarize, content management has two distinct phases: web development and web production. The released version of the web assets defines the content passing from the development side to the production side.

It is essential to treat development and production as distinct activities. First, it subdivides the large problem of creating and serving a web site into two smaller problems. Second, it defines a framework for the various groups of people working on the web site to organize and focus their activities. As the previous example shows, isolating problems is simplified. Third, it identifies the released version as a well-defined intermediate work product. It is simultaneously an output from the development effort, as well as an input to the production side. Fourth, separating the development and production phases with a well-defined deliverable sets the stage for the web operation to scale by hosting multiple production web farms, or by outsourcing the web hosting operation itself.

Common Pitfalls

The release agreement forms a basic operating guideline between the development and production groups. Violating the release agreement causes some common pitfalls to occur.

Sending Untested Content to Production

Deploying changes that haven't been tested is a bad practice. Every effort should be made to avoid sending untested content to production. Sometimes you're lucky and the untested changes turn out to be okay. Eventually, however, luck runs out, and a serious error goes into production. A crisis of some sort ensues, and a major effort is needed to recover from the problem.

That's just the beginning of the problem. There's a deeper and more insidious effect of sending untested changes to production: It undermines the trust between the development and production groups. Sending untested changes to production violates the release agreement because the agreement says that the development group agrees that changes sent to production have been verified to be of good quality. It puts the production group in the awkward position of doubting that any change sent for deployment has been tested.

This doubt is corrosive because it encourages one group to second-guess another. Here is a real-life anecdote. A web production administrator describes the requirement for his web operation. He outlines how he wants to update the production sever to reflect a file deletion on the development side. The consultant says that normal practice is to delete the corresponding file on the production server. The administrator concurs, but he follows up by asking whether, before the file is deleted on the production side, the to-be-deleted file could be archived somewhere "just in case." Of course, this is a natural reaction to previous experiences where unintended file deletions have occurred. His request for an archival copy protects against the scenario that a change is propagated to production, in this case the deletion of a file, but the change turns out to be erroneous.

In spite of the good intentions, the production administrator's approach of keeping informal copies of deleted files is counterproductive in the end. Although this archiving solves some problems, it introduces other larger problems. Suppose recopying a file from the production-side archive fixes a problem. What happens when the subsequent deployment happens? The file will be deleted again! Therefore, the time spent recopying from the archive could have been better spent fixing the problem in the released version and deploying that change. Furthermore, what happens when an error is found in the production web site? Because content potentially comes from two sources, one from the development group and another from the production-side archive, now there are two places to hunt to find the source of the error. The better way to solve the problem is to adhere to the release agreement, which asserts that changes sent to production have been tested.

Making Fixes Directly on the Production Servers

Another common pitfall is to make changes directly on the production server. This is a tempting way to fix mistakes found in production, but it quickly becomes counterproductive. First, the change made in production is risky because the changes are made on a live server. Second, there is no tracking, accountability, or audit trail for the change. Third, it introduces another source of change, and this vastly complicates the tracking problems. For example, if content or logic on the production site is found to be in error, did the change come from the development side or does it come from a manual fix on the production server? Furthermore, additional problems are introduced. How long is the fix supposed to be in place? Is it safe to overwrite the change? When can the change be overwritten? Again, the better way to solve the problem is to adhere to the release agreement and to insist that changes sent to production have been tested.

Continuous Change

Web assets change much more frequently than conventional packaged software. Although both are software assets, web assets are instantly available to its target audience over the web when they are deployed to production. In contrast, conventional packaged software traditionally has a slower means of distribution. Consequently, the time delay between successive releases of packaged software is likely to be greater, often months or years. For example, in packaged software, a user is likely to be surprised if only a month separates versions 1.5 and 1.6. A month is barely enough time for the distribution channel to put version 1.5 into the hands of end-users, so announcing version 1.6 so soon after version 1.5 confuses customers.

Because web assets are delivered to their audience via the web, this encourages frequent releases. Typically, releases occur at least daily, and often more frequently than that. By today's standards, a web site updated only monthly is considered lethargic. Such a site would have difficulty attracting the repeat visitation rate that web managers value so highly. This is true for external public sites and for intranet/extranet sites used within an organization.

When a web site changes frequently, this is equivalent to a succession of releases from the development side. For example, if changes occur hourly, then this is logically equivalent to 24 releases per day. As we'll see in the next section, this doesn't necessarily imply that there is one physical copy sent for each release. Send the incremental changes, instead of sending the entire version.

Database Assets

We define a web asset broadly to include database assets, in addition to file system assets such as files and directories. Database assets include tables, rows, and stored procedures. We take this approach because it is increasingly common for a web server to be associated with an application server. Application servers use both file and database assets. Common application servers include IBM WebSphere, ATG Dynamo, BEA WebLogic, BroadVision One-To-One, and Vignette Lifecycle Presentation Server. When we say that a development group produces periodic, released versions of web assets, we implicitly embrace the creation and maintenance of the database assets that are used by any application servers that run on the production servers. For example, an element of business logic might say that a certain press release will become active at a specific time in the future, and it will be displayed to a particular category of incoming visitors. A row in a database table encodes this business logic by associating an activation time and visitor group code with the press release.

Figure 7.4. shows how a web server, application server, and database server use web assets to create a web presence. The web assets are enlarged in the figure to highlight the combination of file and database assets. Deployment is the process of moving a released version of the web assets to a production server, where both file and database assets move in tandem. This deployment is shown in Figure 7.5.

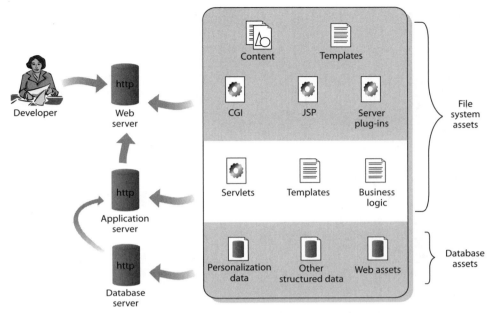

FIGURE 7.4
A web asset broadly includes database assets and file system assets.

Design Considerations

Incremental Changes

Although changes are frequent, the change between successive versions is usually small. We'll refer to the two sides of the deployment as the source and destination sides. We deploy copies of files, directories, rows, and tables from the source side to the destination side. There is a *positive difference* when any of the following conditions are true:

a. The source side has a file, directory, row, or table asset, and the destination side has no corresponding file, directory, row, or table.

b. The source and destination files are different in some prearranged way, such as modification timestamp, file size, file checksum, or file permissions.

c. The source and destination rows are different in some prearranged way, such as value.

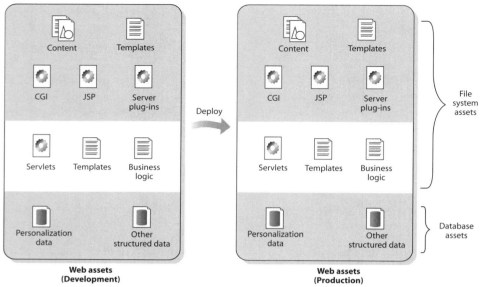

FIGURE 7.5
Deploy file and database assets from development to production in tandem.

There is a *negative difference* when the destination side has a file, directory, row, or table, and the source side has no corresponding file, directory, row, or table.

For positive differences, the destination is populated with the copies of file and directories from the source side. For the negative differences, delete the files and directories on the destination side.

There are different ways of sending changes to production. There are two kinds of deployment, a comparison driven deployment, and a list-driven deployment. In a *comparison-driven deployment*, a hierarchy traversal compares a source-side directory and a destination-side directory. (See Figure 7.6.)

In a *list-driven deployment*, a list governs the transfer of assets from source to destination. Each item on the list corresponds to a difference. If the difference is a positive difference, the asset is copied from the source to the destination. Recall that a positive difference means that the source has an asset that either doesn't exist on the destination, or the destination asset is different in some prearranged way from the source asset. If the difference is a negative difference, the deployment deletes the listed asset from the destination. *Incremental* deployment overlays both positive and negative changes. (See Figure 7.7.)

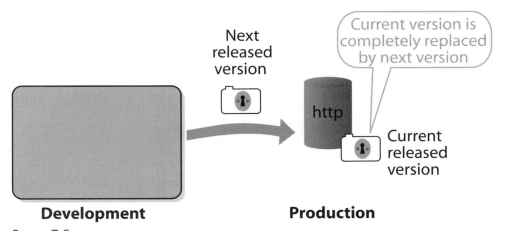

FIGURE 7.6
A comparison-driven deployment incorporates positive and negative differences to move all changes to production from development.

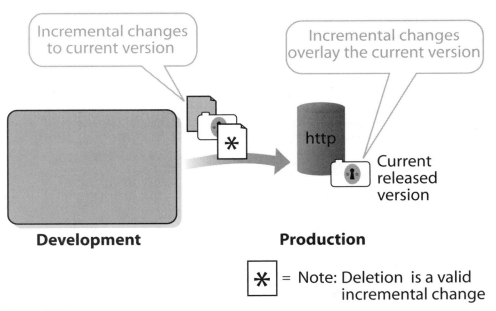

FIGURE 7.7
Incremental deployment overlays positive and negative changes on the production assets.

A special case of list-driven deployment is when the content repository generates the list as the difference between any two areas.[1]

Making Changes Transactional

In a production environment, hardware, software, and network failures inevitably occur. A failure could have many causes, including disk full conditions, broken network links, machine crashes, power failures, and so forth.

Dependencies between web site assets are common. A failure that occurs during deployment of multiple assets with dependencies can be especially problematic. For example, an HTML page references an image. A database record references a sound file. Suppose one asset, `index.html`, refers to an audio asset, `soundbite.ram`, and both files are deployed. If a failure occurs during deployment, one of the files could be sent, while the other isn't. This leads to a broken link, or an orphan asset. Alternatively, a file might be truncated if a network connection breaks during deployment. For instance, the integrity of the production web site is compromised if the file `soundbite.ram` is missing or truncated. The `index.html` page references the missing or incomplete sound file.

A *transactional deployment* scheme preserves the integrity of the production web site in the presence of failures that occur during deployment. When we say that changes are transactionally placed on the production server, we mean that if there are multiple file additions and removals, either the changes appear together, or they do not appear at all.

Under our broad notion of web asset, a transaction could also mean that a row in a relational database table and a file referenced from the row are deployed together, or not at all. Just as in the example of an HTML file that references a media file, a row in a database references a media file. The requirement is the same. Because the row references the media file, the deployment of the row cannot take place without the media file being present. Deploying the pair of assets as a transaction satisfies this requirement.

What Initiates Deployment?

The appropriate time to initiate a deployment depends on the situation, and usually a significant part of the implementation effort revolves around making the deployments happen at the right time.

---

[1] For example, Interwoven's OpenDeploy™ product computes the differences between the previous edition and the staging area, and a deployment uses the result to drive the deployment.

Scheduled Changes

Over the lifetime of a web site, many operations that might involve deployment. Let's describe them, putting the deployment situations in their proper context. There is a periodicity associated with a web site. *Periodic changes* go to production on a schedule known in advance. This is analogous to a conventional printing model where newspapers are published daily, and a magazine is published weekly or monthly. Web sites have similar periodic changes. For example, an online retailer might have weekly merchandise promotions, or an online auctioneer might feature certain categories of goods, perhaps to coincide with the birthday of a famous personality. Or, the promotion might coincide with a national holiday, such as patriotic artifacts to coincide with a July 4 celebration in the U.S. market. Or it could be a purely internally driven dynamic, such as an internal web infrastructure release, to prepare for a subsequent changeover to a fully application-server-driven web site.

The important point regarding deployment is that many periodic events drive the content of a web site. The key is to select the right kind of deployment to produce at that point. For example, some of the events should reflect known-good points, such as a nightly snapshot.

Because periodic changes are known in advance, the web assets associated with them can be sent to production during a convenient time. For example, for some changes to take effect on the web server, the web server is shut down and restarted. Because this can be intrusive, it is best to schedule this kind of deployment to off-peak hours.

On-Demand Changes

Another source of change is on-demand change. *On-demand changes* go to production as soon as possible. An example might be a critical spelling fix or a software patch to an application program module.

Implementing on-demand changes usually requires coordinating with the web production server infrastructure. On-demand changes should be done with the web server shut down or quiescent. For example, network control hardware should divert web traffic away from a designated server, which provides an opportunity for the server to be cycled. Most web servers hold open file handles on pages even when they aren't being actively rendered, thereby making it difficult or impossible for the deployment program to replace a file during heavy use. For example, a home page such as `index.html` of a web site is hit very frequently, and copying a replacement version of that file during peak hours will be unreliable. First, a web server will typically hold a file open with a file descriptor or file handle. Second, the web server may have internally cached the contents of the file, and it may take it a while before it notices that its cached copy has become stale.

Event-Driven Changes

Event-driven changes are initiated by triggering external scripts on events such as submit, publish, create branch, create work area, and so on. Commonly, events such as submitting files to the staging area or publishing an edition initiate further processing. For example, let's suppose that the checking and approval process culminates in files being submitted to the staging area. In some situations, especially for small operations, it is convenient for the submit event to trigger an automatic deployment to a production server. By this technique, approved files that are submitted move from development to production without manual intervention. Alternatively, a larger organization may decide that the submit event will trigger a workflow that manages a combined approval and deployment process. In both examples, the submit event directly or indirectly triggers a deployment.

Script Integration

Certain scripted activities happen before deployment, to prepare for the arrival of web assets at the destination. Other activities occur after deployment, to transition to a full production state. If a failure or error occurs during the deployment, further handling takes place, such as recovery, retry, notification, or some combination of these.

Common Requirements

Let's look at the scripts that run before and after a deployment. Suppose there is a production server farm. Each server in the farm receives a deployment in sequence. Before a deploy commences to a given production server, we run a script that first removes that server from the IP traffic routing, then waits until the server's has become quiescent, and finally shuts down the web and application servers. If the deploy completes successfully, another script runs; it starts the application server, starts the web server, resumes IP traffic routing to the production server, and finally sends an e-mail to the server support group. If the deployment fails, or otherwise returns an error status, then we run a pager notification script, as well as an e-mail notification.

This example illustrates the kinds of activities that occur before and after the deployment itself. We see that the deployment itself is but one component action in an ensemble. There are two additional aspects of the design: success/failure handling and notification.

Handle Success and Failure

Deployment scripts must distinguish the successful case from the failure case. For instance, suppose that before deploying, a pre-deployment script removes a given server machine from the pool of active servers and shuts down the web server. If the subsequent deployment is successful, then another script resumes full production by restarting the web server, and it reinserts the server machine into the active server pool. On the other hand, if there is a failure during the deployment, this triggers recovery steps, such as removing the production server that failed to deploy from the service rotation and possibly initiating a retry sequence for the deployment.

In general, any script associated with a deployment step must be treated as a conditional element with multiple exit states in the overall logic. The successful case is merely one of many possible exit conditions. You should study each script to identify the possible failure paths. For example, the deployment program can exit with an error code because the network connection breaks. Similarly, if Perl code opens files, writes files, copies files, reads files, accesses a database, then any of these operations may exit with an error. As with any program that attempts to handle error cases robustly, the internal logic should record and propagate the exit status.

Notify

Since a significant proportion of deployment activities typically occurs outside of prime business hours, some kind of notification is desirable, on both the success and failure paths. An appropriate medium for notification could be e-mail, paging, or some other means. Determine who should be notified, and specify the contents of the message. On a successful deployment, a summary of the quantity and volume of assets transferred provides a reassurance and a prudent basic check. On a failure notification, the recipient needs to be informed what failed and the severity of the failure, so that appropriate recovery action can be taken. For example, if an entire web server farm shares a common file server, and the deployment fails because the file server fills up in the midst of the deploy, that's a serious failure because the production web site is either incomplete or stale. On the other hand, if deployment fails to one server of many in a large web server farm, that is less serious. One server might refuse to accept the deployment, but the remaining servers have successful deployments. This situation is less urgent because most servers are in production with the correct contents.

A notification infrastructure is essential to make the deployment maintainable on a 24×7 basis. In that infrastructure, workload should be shared by a staff on a rotating basis, so notification on both normal and exceptional events becomes an important part of knowing when things are running smoothly and when an active response is necessary.

Rollback

Rollback is the ability to pick a recent known-good version of the web site and to reset the production web site to that state. Usually rollback is done when a serious error is found on the production web site, and it is more expedient to live with a temporary replacement web site, compared to the associated delays and efforts to remedy the problem. A *known-good* web site is a full snapshot of a given web site that is deemed suitable as a temporary replacement. A *rollback deployment* is a full deployment of a known-good version of web assets to the production web site. We'll refer to the known-good version as the *rollback version*.

As you design a deployment infrastructure, determine whether you need to support the ability to roll back. The primary benefit of rollback lies in the ability to handle errors that propagate to the production web site. All web teams strive to have as few errors as possible; having systematic procedures in place for testing, review, and approval helps to minimize errors. In spite of best efforts, errors sometimes occur, and having the ability to roll back avoids a catastrophic outage.

There are four requirements for invoking a rollback deployment:

   1. At all times, there is a designated rollback version.
   2. The rollback version is available in its entirety, suitable for deployment.
   3. A procedure is in place to institute the rollback.
   4. There is a mechanism to capture a fresh rollback version periodically.

Let's look at these requirements in detail. First, at all times there is some version of the web site that is the designated rollback version. This is because the need for rollback can occur at any time. For a public Internet site that changes many times daily, the rollback version is typically a snapshot from the prior evening. This means that if something goes drastically wrong during the day, the problem can be temporarily fixed by rolling back to last night's version. Although the version is stale, it is usually preferred over the alternative course of action, which is to diagnose and fix the current production version. It can easily take longer to find the root of the problem, than to implement and deploy the repaired assets to production.

Second, the rollback version needs to be available in its entirety, suitable for an immediate comparison-driven full deployment. This eliminates obtaining a rollback version by way of a lengthy compile-and-build step. Similarly, we cannot use a rollback version that requires time-consuming version-control file checkout operations. For example, if parts of the web site need to be checked out of a software configuration management system, and then compiled and rebuilt, this prolongs the outage. Completing a software build typically requires skilled people resources, machine resources, and time. If the outage occurs during working hours, this could easily take a half-hour to accomplish. Otherwise, there's the additional delay in contacting the appropriate people.

Unfortunately, a high-traffic web site cannot tolerate being inoperable for 30 minutes. If the traffic reaches 1,000 hits per minute, this implies 30,000 hits against an inoperable web site. Even if only certain parts of the web site were broken, a delay in restoring a broken web site to a functioning state translates to a diminished web experience for all visitors for that duration. The ability to roll back quickly minimizes the impact on the audience of the web site.

Third, a procedure needs to be in place to institute the rollback that works in concert with supporting scripts and deployment configurations. Typically, we can use a comparison-driven, full deployment, including both positive and negative changes, to restore the production web server to the rollback version.

Fourth, a periodic mechanism needs to create the candidate rollback version snapshots of the web assets. This means that one or more times daily, the production servers synchronize with the staging area, and an edition is created to snapshot the staging area. When this event occurs, all changes in the staging area are pushed to production.

Selecting a Rollback Version

There are many ways to select a known-good version. The most commonly used known-good version is the previous nightly snapshot. This has the benefit of being reasonably timely and fully functional, although close inspection of the contents reveals dated content to the viewer. If the contents change sufficiently rapidly that there's not a convenient way to capture a day-old or possibly one-week-old web site as a designated known-good web site, then you might consider building a special purpose web site. Such a special purpose known-good web site retains the core functionality, but disables time-critical sections for which turning a section off is preferred over stale content. Least useful might be an "under-construction" or "we'll be right back" placeholder pages.

Different parts of a web site can have separate rollback versions. Pure content sections of a web site can be captured daily or even hourly, while software-application driven assets can be captured at designated releases. For example, a commerce site typically has scripts and executables that implement functions such as search, ordering, and account management. These kinds of assets go through a more rigorous release process as compared with graphics and text. The rollback versions of the script and executable assets should be captured at the time that versions are released from the quality assurance process, while the pure content can be captured daily or hourly.

Interestingly, the television broadcast networks have their equivalent of known-good content. When a severe technical problem occurs during a broadcast, we sometimes see a frozen frame of the telecast. Perhaps the audio channel continues, while the picture is frozen. Viewers find a frozen frame of head shots of sportscasters preferable to an unintelligible picture. Another known-good replacement might be a title screen for the program that has been interrupted. Least preferred of all might be a color bar test pattern. The latter is television's equivalent of the "under construction" web page.

Designing a Deployment Infrastructure

Let's walk through the steps in designing a deployment infrastructure. To get started, we answer the following questions:

a. When is a deployment triggered? (Manually—from a user interface—or scheduled? When does this occur? Event-triggered—what's the event?)

b. Where is the source? (What kind of content is moved from development? Does it come from the staging area, an edition, or a change list from a workflow? Is it the entire area, or a subset of files and directories within the area?)

c. Where is the destination? (Are there multiple production servers?)

d. What kind of deployment is it? (Comparison driven or list-driven? Only positive differences or both positive and negative differences sent?)

The answers to these questions provide the raw information from which to begin to articulate a design for the deployment infrastructure. The basic building block is a deployment unit. A *deployment unit* specifies who or what initiates the deployment, when it occurs, and it identifies a source and a destination for the deployment action. For example, a deployment unit might describe how a web producer moves particular files in the `/images` folder on the staging area on-demand, to the corresponding `images` folder on a production web server. Typically, several deployment units together comprise a deployment infrastructure design. For example, another deployment unit might determine how application code is moved into production to update an application server that runs alongside the production web server.

For each deployment unit, we ask additional questions. The answers help us to refine the details of the design.

a. If the deployment is manually initiated who is allowed to initiate it?

b. How is the transfer done? (Encrypted? Transactional?)

c. What notification is done on success? On failure?

d. Is a script run on success? On failure?

e. Is a script run before or after the deployment, either on the development side, or on the production side? Does the web server have any special requirements regarding scripting before or after it receives the assets?

f. Are there database assets to be deployed together with the file assets?

g. How are errors handled? (Notification? Retry?)

h. Who maintains the configuration? (For example, who maintains the list of people to be paged and/or e-mailed with notifications? If a new person joins the group, or leaves the group, how does this affect the permissions and notification?)

Enterprise Deployment Architecture

Requirements

This section describes a deployment infrastructure design that is appropriate for an enterprise-class web operation, with many web sites managed and operated by multiple business units.[2] The organization has strong characteristics of a "state," as introduced in Chapter 3. Each business unit has a formal charter to produce one or more Intranet web sites to facilitate communication and collaboration, both within the business unit, and between business units. A business unit owns each web site. The deployment infrastructure provides a mechanism for the web assets for the particular site to be moved to production either immediately or at a scheduled time. See Figure 7.8.

The deployment design has two sets of requirements. One set of requirements relates to the movement of assets. Note that they are very similar to the ones given in the earlier example.

1. Allow changes to be moved into production at a scheduled time (e.g., off-peak hours).

2. Support the ability of a web manager for the business unit to move specific, urgent files and directory changes to production on-demand, or at a scheduled time in the future.

3. Support the ability to roll back the production web site to a designated known-good version.

4. Take periodic snapshots of the staging area, daily for example, to serve as known-good rollback versions.

Because this solution is used in an enterprise, the second set of requirements relates to administering the people who play different roles in the deployment infrastructure. Formal rules enforced by the organization define the responsibilities of the different participants in the deployment infrastructure. First, the Intranet content consists of independently managed web sites owned by individual business units. Second, within a business unit, the assets are further subdivided into sections. For example, the programming group owns the application code that drives the CGI subsystem, while the content group owns the image and text content. Third, the responsibility for the web presence falls on a business owner, who determines the form and timing of changes to the web site. Fourth, many different individuals play different roles in the overall administration of the infrastructure, and there needs to be a way to allow only particular people to perform certain operations. This contrasts with a small or medium-size web team that typically has more relaxed rules about permissions and access.

---

[2] The organization corresponds to the "Level 4, Transformation" phase described in R. Valdes, et.al., "Web-site deployment and operations," Gartner Group, Strategic Analysis Report, R-07-1162, January 8, 1999.

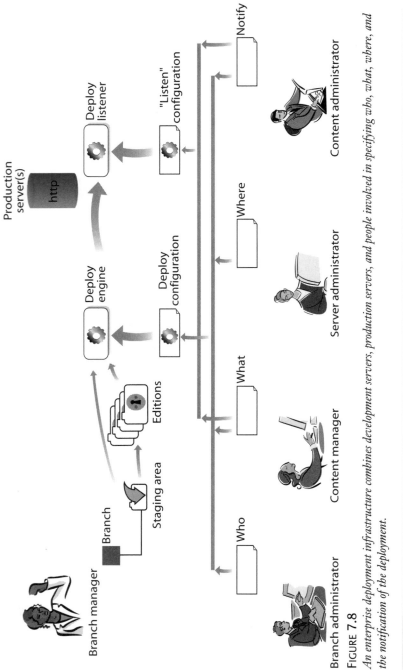

FIGURE 7.8

An enterprise deployment infrastructure combines development servers, production servers, and people involved in specifying who, what, where, and the notification of the deployment.

1. Each business unit is responsible for the following aspects of the deployment infrastructure:

   a. Specify the major subsections of the web assets.

   b. Restrict who is authorized to deploy each section of the web site, on a scheduled or on-demand basis.

   c. Specify the predetermined scheduled times that deployments occur.

2. The network infrastructure group is responsible for the following activities:

   a. For a given business unit, specify the production server that each section of the web site is deployed to.

   b. Specify who is notified, and by what means, for success and failure of each deployment.

   c. Maintain the encryption keys used for the secure deployment.

   d. Write and maintain the scripts that run before and after deployment.

Table 7.1 shows the deployment units, highlighting the division of responsibilities. For an enterprise class deployment implementation, it is essential that responsibilities be clearly defined. For example, the business unit defines the major subdivisions of the web site.

Implementation

A user interacts with the deploy subsystem through a browser-based interface. It validates that precisely one branch has been selected. If not, an error dialog box is popped up. Otherwise, it uses the logged on user, and consults a configuration file (`deploy.cfg`) that specifies for each branch, who is authorized to drive a deploy, and which deployment names to drive. The deployment names are specified in another configuration file. Each deployment name specifies subdirectories within the branch's staging area, and specifies where to deploy them. Additionally, exclusion rules, permission handling, and symbolic link handling logic, can be specified in this file. See Figure 7.9.

The pull-side of the deploy uses a configuration file to specify from which push-side deploy hosts to receive deployments from, what port to use, and which key file it should use to compute its private key for encryption.

The implementations of "deploy immediately" and "one-time scheduled" share a common implementation. First, there is a common infrastructure to determine whom to notify, upon the completion of the deployment. Both the immediate and scheduled deploys consult a common set of notification configuration files. This makes maintenance of the deployment script easier, and makes maintenance of the configuration files more straightforward.

TABLE 7.1
An Enterprise Class Deployment Infrastructure Specifying the Responsibilities of the Content and Network Administrators.

Name	Description	What is Deployed	When Initiated	Who Initiates	Deploy Mode	Script Intergration
1. Regularly scheduled	Move normal changes to production server, according to schedule.	All changes in staging area, within a designated section of the web site. (Business unit is responsible for defining sections of web site.)	According to schedule (Business unit is responsible for defining schedule.)	Automatic job (Network infrastructure group is responsible for making sure jobs run on time.)	Comparison-driven, positive and negative changes.	Before and after deploy, scripts cycle web server. Notification on success and failure. (Network infrastructure group maintains scripts.)
2. One-time scheduled	Move normal changes to production server, one-time scheduled event.	Files and directories on change list.	According to schedule (Business unit determines who is allowed to one-time deploy.)	Manually created job (Network infrastructure group is responsible to make sure job runs on time.)	Comparison-driven, positive and negative changes.	Before and after deploy, scripts cycle web server. Notification on success and failure. (Network infrastructure group maintains scripts.)
3. Immediate	Move urgent changes to production server as soon as possible.	Files and directories on change list.	On-demand	Web producer, via user interface (Business unit determines who is allowed to do this.)	List-driven, positive changes. Transactional.	Before and after deploy, scripts cycle web server. Notification on success and failure. (Network infrastructure group maintains scripts.)

TABLE 7.1
An Enterprise Class Deployment Infrastructure Specifying the Responsibilities of the Content and Network Administrators. (Continued)

Name	Description	What is Deployed	When Initiated	Who Initiates	Deploy Mode	Script Intergration
4. Rollback	Roll back the production web site to a predetermined known-good version. Support rollback by defining the rollback versions regularly.	Rollback version, typically all of a particular edition.	On-demand	Production manager, via user interface (Business unit determines who is allowed to do this.)	Comparison-driven, positive and negative changes. Transactional.	Before and after deploy, scripts cycle web server. Notification on success and failure. (Network infrastructure group maintains scripts.)

Figure 7.9 shows how each menu-driven deploy causes a temporary per-deploy configuration file to be created on-the-fly from the who, what, where, and notify configuration files. Let's walk through an example to see how this works. When a user selects

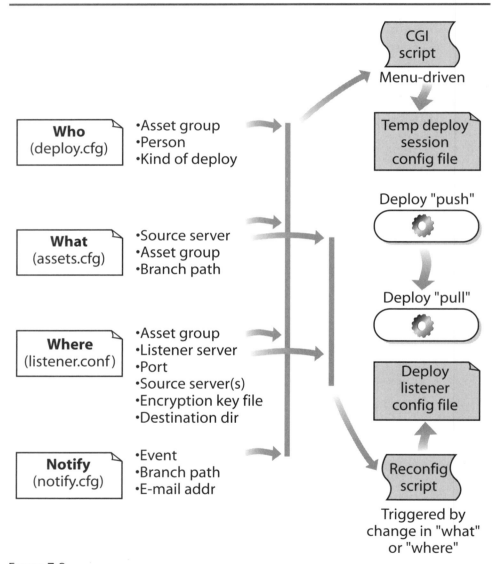

FIGURE 7.9

A deployment infrastructure specifies who is allowed to deploy, what they're able to deploy, where they deploy to, and who is to be notified on success and failure.

an edition, for instance, and uses the deploy-now menu item, the CGI script knows who the user is, and knows which branch the selected edition is on. First the "who" file is consulted to determine which asset groups that user is authorized to deploy. Second, the "what" file narrows down further which asset groups correspond to that branch. Third, the "where" file is read to determine, for that asset group, which listening servers will accept deployments from that server. The "where" file contains additional information to specify the port, the encryption key, and the destination directory for the deployment. A one-time use deploy configuration file is created for each asset group, and a deployment is started for each one. Because the listening sides of the deployment read the same "where" and "what" configuration files, we're assured that the deployment will go through without mismatch. Finally, the "notify" file is used to generate the appropriate e-mail notification regarding the deployment.

Summary

Deployment serves the business critical function of moving finished and approved web assets from development onto one or more production servers. Often underestimated in its importance, a deployment infrastructure binds together the web assets, the hardware and network resources, the people, and the business processes into a coherent whole. A deployment infrastructure operates around the clock, and the design decisions that it embodies reaches across organizations. A well-designed structure facilitates a smooth running operation during times of normal functioning, as well as making it a straightforward task to identify and isolate problems when things go wrong.

Practitioner's Checklist

1. Identify deployment units that specify who or what initiates the deployment, when it occurs, and what is a source and a destination for the deployment action.
2. Use regularly scheduled deployment driven by an automatic job to move normal changes to the production server.
3. Use immediate deployment to move urgent changes to production.
4. Arrange to have a rollback edition available at all times for use in rollback deployment.

CHAPTER EIGHT

MULTIPLE WEB INITIATIVES

Chaos often breeds life,

when order breeds habit. *—Henry Brooks Adams*

Executive Summary

Multiple, concurrent web initiatives require careful arrangement of people and assets to effectively achieve business goals. Delineate a web property under the responsibility of an organization with a well-defined charter. Follow the WSE paradigm (work area, staging area, and edition), to define a branch of development that consists of a staging area, and associated work areas and editions.

Introduction

Most organizations engage in multiple web initiatives simultaneously. There's too much to do in so little time. Alternate sales channels need to be explored. Partnerships need to be supported via an extranet. New product lines need to be launched. Field operations need to be more tightly integrated into the corporate Intranet, while simultaneously requiring more autonomy in localizing their offerings. A second-generation revamp of the core web property needs to be completed, tested, and brought online.

These situations share a common feature: a development effort with a single-minded business purpose. Numerous content contributors, developers, reviewers,

135

testers, and business owners strive toward an overarching business objective. A common objective necessitates a cohesive timeline and pace of work that drives the effort.

Building an effective web development operation relies critically on defining clear business objectives. Success depends on linking the external objectives with the internal organization of people and assets. The people in the development organization might include contractors and partners outside the formal organization who contribute content nonetheless. The assets being developed comprise the web property. The goal is to strive to find an alignment of the business objective, the organization chartered to attain the objective, and a careful delineation of the web property under the organization's control.

To define the web property, create a development environment to tie together the objective, the people, and the assets. Within the WSE paradigm, define a *branch of development* as a single staging area, together with associated work areas where developers undertake tasks, and editions where site-level versions are maintained. A good *branch structure* minimizes interference between developers as they work on tasks concurrently. This makes work processes efficient, by eliminating extra steps in updating and synchronizing content from one branch to another.

This chapter introduces the concept of logically independent web sites, and the notion of task overlap. It describes four patterns of branch structure that form fundamental building blocks for more complex structures. You can use this fragment to choose an appropriate branch structure.

Overview

Picking a branch structure requires a combination of different kinds of knowledge. First, become familiar with the assets being moved under content management and how individuals and teams modify content. Learn the organization structure of the teams, the timelines for typical changes, and analyze the extent to which groups make changes that overlap in time. Web project managers and the web administrators possess this knowledge. A considerable amount of information is needed to choose the right branch structure. Typically, a meeting between the implementers, web managers, and web technical leads will provide you with the best forum for exchanging information. Use a big whiteboard, corral a block of time in the morning, and bring a willingness to ask questions.

Here's an overview of the steps to determine a good branch structure. First, identify the logically independent web sites; we'll define this term shortly. Second, within each logically independent web site, determine the overlap between tasks performed in the web site, and the release times of the tasks. We'll define the notion of task overlap and release time in the following section. If there's little overlap between tasks, use a single branch. If the overlapping tasks have similar release times, use a single branch. If there's much overlap or the release times differ greatly, consider using a long-term/ short-term branch pattern, grouping tasks of similar release times into the same branch. Finally, under special conditions, it makes sense to subdivide a logically independent web site even further, into a web site or other collection of assets that does not constitute a functional web site. With this preview of the procedure, let's start from the beginning and define the important concepts.

Concepts

Logically Independent Web Site

A *logically independent web site* consists of the web assets to render a functionally complete web site. For example, a static HTML web site is logically independent because HTML files and images render a functionally complete web site. For a CGI-based web site, a functionally complete web site additionally needs the CGI programs and scripts. For an application-server-based web site, the logical web site includes all the resources required by the application server, including the template files, the configuration files, and the servlet/JSP source code files. In each of these cases, identify the assets required to render a functionally complete web site.

Developers working on a logical web site can release content changes more or less independently from other content outside the logical web site. From a development perspective, the web site is separate. Ask yourself the following question: What assets need to be gathered to transfer a functionally complete web property to another development group? Your answer is a logically independent web site.

There are few, if any links from outside a logical web site into a logically independent web site. The inbound links, if any, are to defined and stable pages. For example, a press-release logical web site of a web site has few inbound links if other logical web sites of the web site point to the index page, or to a well-known URL from which all press releases can be rendered. On the other hand, it is less independent if other logical web sites point directly to press-release pages. (The inbound links can be thought of as the "API" of the logical web site.)

Task Overlap

A *task* consists of a set of interrelated changes to web content. Table 8.1 shows some examples of tasks.

Task overlap measures how much the interval demarcated by the start and finish time of a task overlaps with other changes occurring simultaneously on the web site. Ask the following questions: How many developers modify the content in the logically independent web site? What kinds of changes are made? How often are the changes made? Measure from the time a task begins to the time when the changes for the task

TABLE 8.1
Examples of Tasks

Task	Interesting Feature
a. A single developer makes an HTML change.	Task is independent.
b. A web designer and a graphic designer collaborate on new pages.	Two developers collaborate on same task. Sub-tasks are complementary.
c. A developer changes the logic in C++ files to fix a bug.	Task is independent.
d. Several marketing managers create press releases, all of which are scheduled to go-live on the same day.	Tasks are all scheduled to go live at the same time.

go into production. Count the time to implement the change, the time to review the change, the time to approve the change, and the time spent waiting before going into production. Compare that to other changes still in development. A single branch is adequate when there's limited task overlap.

Most web sites change frequently, making task overlap the rule rather than the exception. On a given day it wouldn't be surprising to have the following tasks overlap. One task seeks to insert a new press release. Another task revamps the look-and-feel of the web site. A third task fixes a memory leak in the C++ source code for an ISAPI plug-in.

With overlapping tasks, determine whether the changes will be released at the same time or not. Changes for tasks with different release times should be kept separate to reduce interference. Changes interfere with one another when one change is complete and ready for approval or movement to production, but another change in the same work area isn't complete and hence prevents the first change from being approved or deployed to production.

There are different ways of keeping the changes separate. The simplest is to put changes for a task into separate work areas. A common pattern—the time-slot pattern—keeps changes in a work area. Appendix C describes this pattern in more detail.

Basic Branch Patterns

This section introduces three common branch patterns and a fourth special pattern that finds occasional use:

1. Single-branch pattern
2. Agency pattern (multiple independent branches)

3. Long-term/short-term pattern

4. Dependent-branch pattern

These patterns form the fundamental building blocks of more complex branch structures. Though they seem simple, applying these patterns requires a solid understanding of the concepts introduced earlier.

Single-Branch Pattern

The most common branch structure is the single-branch configuration. Logically independent web content goes into this configuration. (See Figure 8.1.) Use the results of the task overlap analysis to define a development flow consistent with a single staging area. Arrange to keep the task overlap relatively small. For example, all tasks should start and complete within a week or a few days. In contrast, the single-branch pattern doesn't apply when half the web team works on a major revamp of the web site, while the other half pushes out incremental fixes and regularly scheduled content changes. There is significant task overlap in this situation.[1]

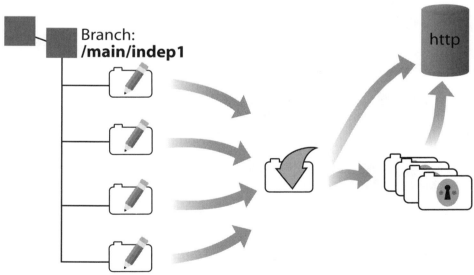

FIGURE 8.1
Logically independent web content goes into a single-branch configuration.

---

[1] The long-term/short-term branch pattern discussed in the next section would be more appropriate in this situation.

Determine the logically independent web content that goes into a branch, and analyze the workflow to identify typical tasks and the overlap between them.

Work Area Configurations

A straightforward approach for organizing the work areas is to arrange for a single task to occur within a work area. In this situation, web developers work independently, or small teams consisting of an HTML developer and an artist collaborate on a task. Placing a task in its own work area minimizes the potential to have conflicts that adversely affect the functionality of the web site; at the same time, isolating the changes facilitates the review and approval process.

Let's revisit the task examples introduced in Table 8.1. Examples (a) and (c) involve a developer working independently; there is a work area for each task. In example (b), a web designer and a graphic artist collaborate on new pages, so have them use a single work area. It makes sense for them to work in the same work area because their changes don't interfere. For example, the web designer will change the HTML, while the artist will change the images. In example (d), the marketing managers make changes independently, but because all of their changes go-live on the same day, and because their changes don't interfere, putting the work in a single work area facilitates the review and deployment of the combined changes.

Option A: Per-Project Work Area

It is quite common to have a single developer or a small group work closely together on interrelated changes that are submitted at the same time. They are interrelated because the assets reference one another, or they use one another. For example, when an HTML developer and a graphic artist develop assets, the HTML code might refer to an image. Similarly, Perl code might use a related Perl module. In this situation, it makes sense to use a separate work area for each such task. (See Figure 8.2.)

After the changes for a project have been submitted, the work area can be reused for the next project. That's why it often makes sense to give each developer a separate work area. In this case, use a work area for a succession of nonoverlapping projects.

If a single developer has multiple ongoing projects, where the changes from one have different submission times, then it may make sense for that developer to have several work areas. For example, in Figure 8.2, Randall has two work areas that he can use for changes that he needs to keep separate because they have different due dates.

Option B: Per-Time-Slot Work Area

In another common situation, content has a strong time dependence. For example, a press release must go-live on a specific day, or a product promotion must begin and end on specific days. In this situation, it sometimes makes sense to define one work

Branch:
/main/ecomm/longterm

FIGURE **8.2**
When a single developer, or a small group work closely together on related changes, it makes sense to configure a branch to have a work area per project.

area per day, with 31 work areas, each corresponding to a day of a month. For example, a work area called, "day12" contains all content scheduled to go to production on the upcoming 12th of the month.

In the simplified usage of this technique shown in Figure 8.3, there is a work area per day of the week.

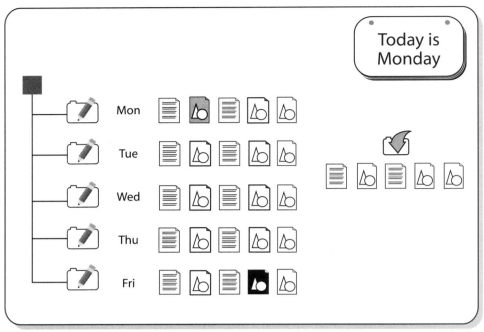

FIGURE 8.3
When web content goes into production on a predetermined daily time schedule, configure the branch with enough work areas to cover the scheduling cycle.

Agency Pattern

Use the agency pattern for multiple, logically independent web sites. (See Figure 8.4.) The pattern gets its name because web development agencies produce web sites for many clients. Since each client's web site is independent from each other, each web site becomes a project onto itself. To keep each project separate, each project uses a different branch. Although we see this pattern with agencies, this pattern occurs in other situations as well.

For example, let's take the case of a web site for a consumer retail web site that has a single point of entry through a corporate homepage. The web development team has detailed discussions about a corporate Web site, along with analysis of the web content and work cycles. They find that the corporate web site can be decomposed into two logically independent web sites for the corporate information section. The latter includes press releases and job listings, distinct from the e-commerce section of the corporate web site. With two logically independent web sites, one for the static section and another for the application-server-driven e-commerce web site, the two

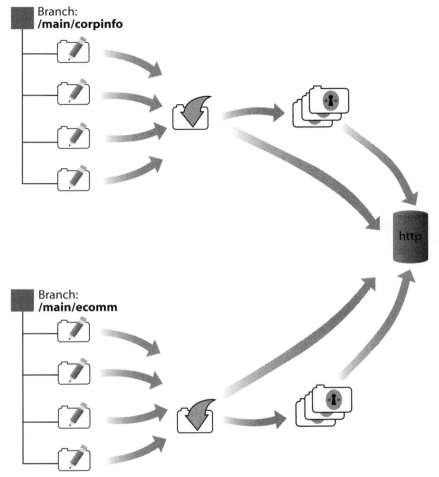

FIGURE 8.4
The agency pattern partitions content into logically independent web sites.

development efforts avoid being trapped in lockstep. The independent information section and the e-commerce sections of the web site use separate content, graphics, and application logic. Different groups of developers develop content, with distinct review and approval processes.

To use the agency pattern, identify the logically independent web sites by studying the external look of the web site. Gain an understanding of the internal organization of the content and the teams that develop the content. Find a logical web site that satisfies the independence criteria, and assign it to its own branch. Developers should work in assigned branches and stay out of other branches. This is the agency pattern.

Short-Term/Long-Term Branch Pattern

Use the long-term/short-term pattern when there's a long-term web development effort going on concurrently with short-term changes to a web site. (See Figure 8.5.) When changes for the long-term branch overlap with changes for the short-term branch, the changes cannot go to production together. Split the development efforts by introducing separate branches.

The impetus to introduce separate branches stems from the impracticality of keeping ongoing changes confined in a work area. Changes tend to propagate beyond the confines of a work area. First, when changes occur in gradual steps over an extended period of time, incremental steps need to be version controlled. Introduce a branch to hold the work products. For instance, a group of web developers undertakes a multi-week effort to revamp the look-and-feel of the corporate information site. The high degree of task overlap recommends the use of a separate branch. A branch gives the ability to use the staging area to integrate intermediate work products, while the work areas hold changes that require additional development and testing before they are ready for integration.

Second, when different teams make changes, the separate changes need to be version controlled in stages. If changes for a given task cannot be kept in a work area, then we ask whether the changes will be released at the same time. For example, suppose both a press release and a bug fix to the search engine must go out tomorrow morning. Two separate teams do the changes, and each team makes their changes in separate work areas. By doing this, each team gets their work reviewed and approved separately. We don't care in which order they complete their tasks. Eventually, the work is integrated, and the changes move to production. If the changes overlap, but are going to production at the same time, then a single branch is sufficient.

Dependent Branch Pattern

In the dependent branch pattern, a branch contains a set of web assets that aren't logically independent. (See Figure 8.6.) For example, the /images directory or the /cgi-bin directory are kept in a branch all to themselves. In particular, a branch that contains all the image assets, but nothing else, doesn't constitute a functioning web site. Use this pattern when there's a compelling reason to subdivide into branches what otherwise would be an independent web site:

1. The volume of assets exceeds the amount that reasonably wants to be kept in a single branch.
2. There is a need to factor out assets for a common subsystem.
3. There is a strong organizational requirement to separate the assets.
4. There is a need to version control assets separately within a subbranch.

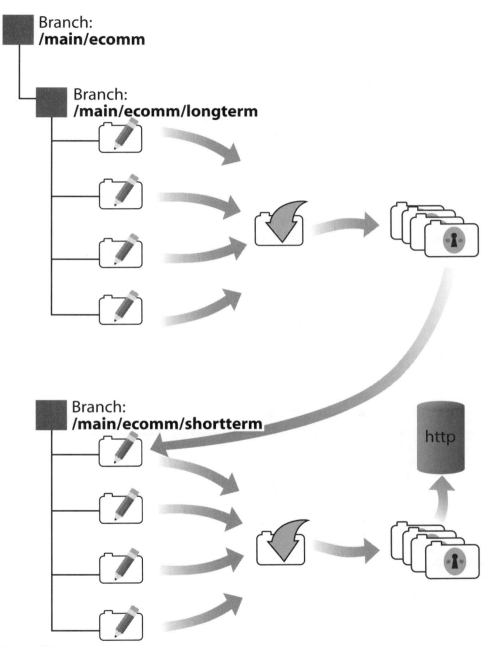

FIGURE 8.5
Use the long-term/short-term branch pattern when tasks overlap within a logically independent web site.

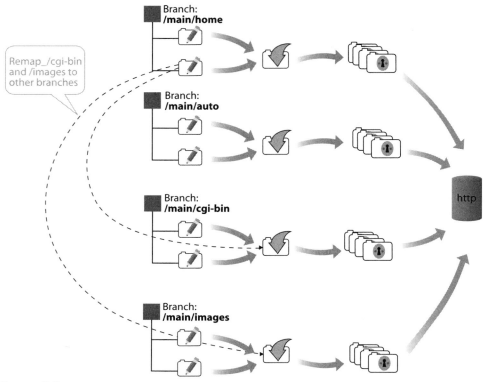

FIGURE 8.6
The dependent branch pattern remaps references to other branches.

With a *super-large web site*, the assets that are logically independent exceed in volume what you'd want to manage as a single branch. For example, many assets in a branch means that work area update time increases. To keep operation times within reasonable bounds, subdividing a super-large web site into manageable dependent branches can be a viable solution.

Sometimes several logically independent web sites use a common subsystem, such as images or cgi-bin. In this situation, you'd prefer not to replicate copies of each of these subsystems into each branch. Factor out the common subsystem as a dependent branch.

Occasionally, organizations divide responsibilities of subparts of a web site purposefully, and they want to reflect that in the organization of the assets. For example, a CGI development group focuses solely on CGI assets, while a separate content development group produces HTML assets. Ordinarily, the logically independent web site principle suggests keeping those subsystems together in a single branch, to facilitate testing, quality assurance, and approval of the integrated web site. By separating these subsystems into branches, and by placing restrictions on who can make changes in the branches, an organization assures itself, for instance, that HTML changes originate solely from the HTML branch.

It's best to form a dependent web site branch to perform additional versioning when a subsystem has content that needs to be versioned at fine-grained checkpoints. For example, a file might go through an approval procedure with multiple reviewers. Checkpoint the file before the review starts. Then, changes resulting from the first review are checkpointed by submitting to the subbranch, and similarly for the second review. At any stage of the process, versions of the file are available for comparison and rollback. When the reviews are completed, propagate the file from the subbranch to the upper branch.

Identifying Branch Patterns

We now have the tools to determine the branch structure. First, identify the logically independent web sites. If there is more than one logically independent web site, then each such web site is treated as in the agency pattern. Each logically independent web site corresponds to a project within the agency.

Investment bank identifies logically independent web sites

An investment bank uses their intranet to disseminate information internally. Each of the hundreds of business units typically hosts one or more web sites on servers scattered throughout the firm. Each business unit develops, controls, maintains, and deploys its content independently from the other business units. As the information technology group sets up a content management infrastructure, they determine that they're playing the role of a web agency, and that each business unit should own a branch to contain the web assets for the business unit.

Second, within each logically independent web site, determine the task overlap. If there is little or no task overlap, then put the logically independent web site into a single branch. If there is some overlap of tasks within a logically independent web site, determine whether the content changes for the tasks go to production at or nearly at the same time. For example, they all go once a week, or twice a week, or there are daily changes. Define the work areas on the branch so that the tasks can be grouped effectively. For instance, if a developer's task is to change the underpinnings of the web site, and the web site is broken while the changes are done, then it makes sense to isolate those changes into a work area of its own.

Small web development group maintains subsection of corporate web site

A life insurance company has an online presence to improve customer service for the many aspects of its business. One web development group maintains the 401K benefits administration section of their web site that primarily serves plan administrators at the client companies. Their section of the corporate web site is logically independent from the rest of the site. The development group consists of a handful of application developers. Contractors working out of the marketing communications group contribute graphic assets. A major revision of the application code is released yearly, coupled with minor updates to application logic and look-and-feel changes scattered throughout the year. Because the frequency of minor updates is low, and most of the changes occur at the annual release, the development group finds that the single-branch structure adequately meets their needs.

If on the other hand, the tasks can be grouped into daily "buckets," then a work area structure corresponding to the time-slot approach might be appropriate.

Online commerce site has predetermined content launch dates

At an online commerce site, product marketers need web assets to be staged to production at a predetermined time, and there's a corresponding need to remove those assets at another predetermined time. For example, a product promotion launches seven days before Valentine's Day, and is replaced by another promotion on February 14. Another product marketer launches a promotion in a different area of the site the Friday before Valentine's Day, and is torn down on the following Monday. The requirement for predetermined launch and tear down dates of overlapping marketing campaigns recommends the use of the time-slotted work area approach.

If the tasks have a high degree of overlap, and have very different release times, then consider using the short-term/long-term branch pattern. For example, a very common situation is to have one group of developers working on a long-term web site revamping, such as converting from an HTML/CGI structure to an application-server-based implementation. At the same time, the existing HTML/CGI web site undergoes continual and frequent updates to run the business, until the switchover to the application server happens. If we consider the long-term conversion project to be a task, then it overlaps with the smaller short-term tasks required to maintain the existing web site. Of course, none of the application-server changes can move to production until that project is complete, which necessitates that we separate the long-term and short-term changes on different branches.

Online retailer separates weekly vs. daily site development

A click-and-mortar retailer has weekly and twice-weekly pushes of content that involve multiple HTML developers and artists. The application development group submits code changes to the commerce engine every week or so. At the same time, reactive changes to content are initiated, reviewed, and deployed within the span of a few hours, and at the rate of up to ten changes daily. Because of the significant degree of overlap between the daily tasks and the weekly tasks, it makes sense to institute a two-branch structure. The daily changes go into the short-term branch, and the weekly, twice weekly, and application code changes go into the long-term branch.

Finally, determine whether any of the special conditions listed below warrant applying the dependent branch pattern to the further subdivide of any single-branch patterns.

Web development group factors their CGI assets

An online catalog retailer has expanded its web operation into several lines of business, but it has decided to maintain a common base of application logic embodied in its CGI assets. The content assets of the web site have been separated into logically independent subsections of the site, which reside in separate branches. The exception is that the CGI assets have been factored and placed in a separate branch. The CGI code is tested and reviewed in its own branch. Test pages and corresponding test content reside in the CGI branch. Content development in the other branches use a proxy daemon and remap rules to refer CGI references to the latest-and-greatest CGI content in the staging area of the CGI branch. Full testing of a given web site occurs on a pre-production test server, which combines the non-CGI and CGI content in a test web site. The need to factor the CGI assets justifies subdividing the web assets according to the dependent branch pattern, along with the proxy remap rules.

Let's summarize the steps in choosing a branch structure:

1. Identify logically independent web sites.
2. Within each logically independent web site:

   a. Determine the overlap between tasks performed in the web site, and the release times of the tasks.

    b. If there's little overlap between tasks, use a single branch.

    c. Else, if the overlapping tasks have similar release times, use a single branch.

    d. If there's significant overlap or the release times differ greatly, consider using the long-term/short-term branch pattern, grouping tasks of similar release times into the same branch.

3. For each logically independent web site, determine if the situation warrants a further subdivision into dependent web sites. Subdivide in the following cases:

    a. The volume of assets exceeds the amount that reasonably wants to be kept in a single branch (i.e., super-large web site).

    b. There is a need to factor out assets for a common subsystem.

    c. There is a strong organizational requirement to separate the assets.

    d. There is a need to version control assets separately within a subbranch.

If any of the above are true, subdivide into dependent web site branches. Otherwise, stay with the single branch.

Example—Using Branches in a Dot-Com Company

Let's apply what we've learned to an example. We have a dot-com company that produces a web site that provides answers to common questions about home, auto, travel, and work. Home, auto, travel, and work constitute four major sections in the web site. For example, the auto section answers the question, "How do I jump start a car with a dead battery?" We call this question and answer a topic. Each topic consists of one to five HTML pages, and up to ten images. Each of the four sections contains several hundred topics, and is growing.

The production staff is organized functionally: editorial produces the copy, art creates the artwork, and web assembles and maintains the web assets. In addition, a senior web producer oversees each major section, with web producers for subsections. Producers meet regularly to decide on new topics, which section will produce the topic, whether a topic should be moved, and which topics will be updated.

Currently ten topics are added to the site weekly, and about 40 existing topics are updated weekly, either from internal reviews or from customer suggestions from the feedback page. A new topic takes between one to four weeks to go from concept to final stage, and an update to an existing topic takes from ten minutes to one day, from inception to final revision.

Arrange Branches into Logically Independent Web Sites

The first step is to identify the logically independent web sites. Based on our description of the web site, we need to keep the HTML code and the graphics together if we're to have a complete and functioning web site. In other words, we define the logically independent web site as the content that combines the HTML pages, and the artwork that the HTML references. However, because of the way that the web site content is topically divided into home, auto, travel, and work, we propose to define each topical division as a logically independent web site. This gives us four branches (home, auto, travel, and work), each holding a logically independent web site. See Figure 8.7.

In arriving at the branch structure in Figure 8.7, we've made the determination that we don't need another integration branch to reassemble the logically independent web sites. Had the organization had a dedicated group whose charter is to coordinate the integration of assets from the subbranches into an integration branch for review, testing, and approval, an integration branch may then have been appropriate. Instead, each independent web site is tested and approved separately. Pre-production integration occurs on a pre-production server for final approval and load testing.

Creating Departmental Branches Isn't Appropriate

Notice that we have chosen not to split the web site along department lines, because that approach to decomposition wouldn't have given us a functioning web site in each branch. None of the special conditions that justify introducing the dependent branch pattern applies in our situation. For example, the volume of the assets isn't so large as to justify subdividing the content. Similarly, the departments aren't so rigid and compartmentalized to warrant going to a dependent branch structure.

Had we used the dependent branch structure, we'd have to introduce a proxy daemon and remap rules, or we'd have had to institute procedures to migrate content from a dependent subbranch to an integration branch in order to review and test changes. The effect of the latter would make the review and approval process inconvenient, because potential reviewers wouldn't be able to see artwork in the context of the HTML that refers to it, and vice versa. (See Figure 8.8.) For example, suppose that a producer in the client's company has drawn up a proposed branch structure that looks as follows:

- Main
- Editorial
- Art
- HTML

This proposed structure makes review and approval cumbersome. In part, this is because this partitioning doesn't give us a logically independent web site. For example, suppose there's a new topic on how to tie a bow tie. We'll require some artwork showing the steps to tie a bow tie, and we'll have some HTML content for the procedure. If artwork is created in the art branch, and the HTML is created in the HTML branch, then each will be only viewed in isolation. We'd have to delay the approval until the content has been submitted, and copied to the main branch to see how the graphics elements look against each other, and how they fit with the overall page layout.

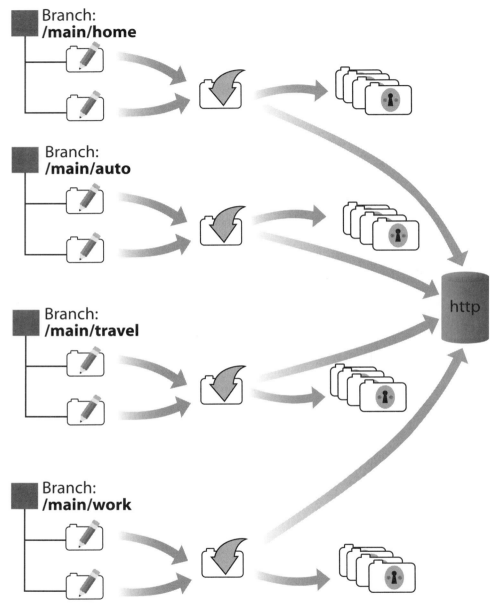

FIGURE 8.7
Separate independent web site content across separate branches when volume constraints dictate.

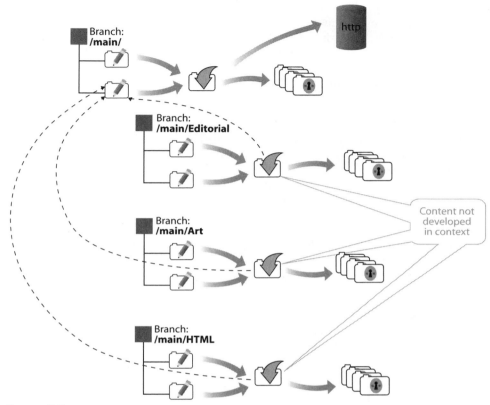

FIGURE 8.8

Dividing content by departments, where the individual branches aren't functionally complete, is a common mistake because content isn't developed in context and the review is cumbersome.

Overuse of Branches

As with any tool or concept, it is possible to overuse branches. The key to proper use of branches lies in carefully following the principle of dividing assets into logically independent web sites. Most circumstances of branch overuse stems from ignoring the idea that each branch should encompass a logically independent web site. Check that the contents on each branch essentially functions as a standalone web site, unless one of the exception conditions applies (3(a–d), in the branch design steps).

Determine Task Overlap

The second step is to determine the task overlap, and relate that to the release of content to production. Find out the typical content development cycle. From the earlier description, we see that new items sometimes have a long gestation period, up to four weeks, whereas changes sometimes happen over a matter of days. This means that there is a sizable overlap of the tasks. We have two choices. We can either arrange for a long-term change to reside in a work area and for it to be submitted only when it has been approved and it is ready to go into production, or we can move to a long-term/short-term branch pattern.

Here's an example that illustrates the decision that we'd make. Suppose we have a one-week effort to write the topic on bow ties, but at the same time, we need to make a quick update to "How do I jumpstart a car with a dead battery?" The latter change needs to be expedited to the production web site in two hours. If the bow-tie project changes involve a small handful of developers, they can probably arrange to make their changes in a single work area. In addition, the changes would be reviewed and approved in the work area. If we can make this work, then the jumpstart topic can be implemented in a new or existing work area. After review and approval, the jumpstart changes are submitted to the staging area for the branch, and moved into production. This arrangement is shown in Figure 8.9. This works when a small team of develop-

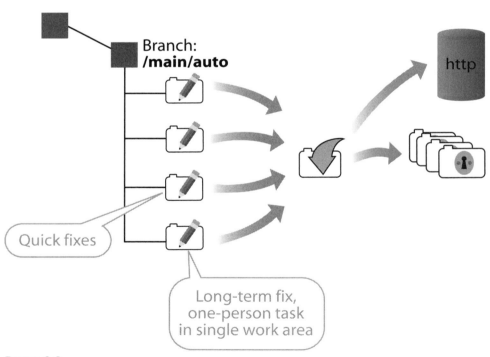

FIGURE 8.9

Use the single-branch pattern when changes for a task are contained in a single work area despite significant overlap between tasks.

ers works closely together, and when the amount of task overlap is relatively small. As we've described this situation, quick fixes move within hours, whereas so-called long-term fixes move within a week. For a task overlap much greater than that, a two-branch structure should probably be recommended over the single-branch structure.

If on the other hand, the bow-tie project involves a larger team with multiple integration steps, it may no longer be the case that we can justify keeping all the changes in a single work area for the duration of the project. For example, the bow-tie project might have a CGI component. Juggling the CGI changes and the overlapping tasks in a single branch would probably lead to confusion, so a two-branch structure—a long-term/short-term branch structure—would be a superior solution in this situation. (See Figure 8.10)

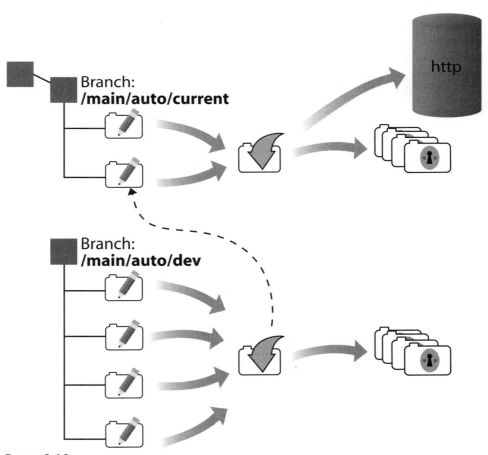

FIGURE 8.10
Use the long-term/short-term branch structure when a logically independent web site has overlapping tasks with very different release times.

To summarize, we examine how the dot-com's web site is organized. We determine that the web content is subdivided into broad topics—home, auto, travel, and work. Each such topic area gives a functioning web site that satisfies the logically independent web site property. Within each topic's web site, we determine that tasks overlap and that the release times for the tasks differ enough to warrant going to a long-term/short-term structure.

Dependent Web Sites

This section describes in more detail a technique to restore virtualization for dependent web sites. The technique involves configuring a proxy daemon. This technique can be used when a very large web site is a logically independent web sites in its entirety, and it turns out that it is too large to be managed as a single branch. For example, a super-large e-commerce and extranet web site contains millions of assets, and there's no reasonable way to subdivide the web site to yield smaller functioning subparts. For the sake of argument, let's say that a million assets is more than a single branch can reasonably hold, given the need to do normal operations such as get-latest, submit, and so forth. How can such a super-large web site be accommodated?

Here's the answer. A dependent web site is partially functional as a standalone web site, but portions of the site contain links to other parts of the super-large web site. Use a mechanism so that when a link cannot be found, the web server "fails over" to another branch. By this means, the web site appears to be a logically complete whole.

Summary

We've introduced the concepts of logically independent work area and task overlap. These concepts help us understand three common branch patterns: single-branch patterns, agency patterns, and short-term/long-term patterns. By examining the content of a physical web site, and by taking into account the work patterns and timelines for changes, we can map out the logically independent sub-web sites of the physical web site. Once we have the logical web sites, the work patterns help us to determine whether a single-branch pattern, agency pattern, or the short-term/long-term branch pattern fits our situation.

Practitioner's Checklist

1. Identify logically independent web site.
2. Determine if conditions warrant multiple branches.
3. Design work area structure for each branch.
4. Validate branch design by walking through usage scenarios with your client.

Part Three

DESIGN AND IMPLEMENTATION

CHAPTER NINE

Using Web Content Management for Globalization

Every shoe fits not every foot. —*Proverb*

Executive Summary

Business realities increasingly demand that companies globalize their web properties. We use the techniques we've learned to design a web content management infrastructure for a company's globalization initiative. We identify the asset types, define the primary work cycles, design the deployment infrastructure, introduce a branch structure to support multiple initiatives, and design a content entry subsystem using templates.

Introduction

An organization exploits the full potential of the Internet by globalizing its web properties. It reaches customers, partners, and suppliers in a particular region by appropriate use of language and culture. We refer to the characteristics of language and culture that correspond to a region as the *locale*. A *globalized* web property uses locale-specific knowledge to both present information and to request input in region-friendly ways. For instance, times, dates, monetary amounts, numbers, addresses, telephone numbers, and fonts should follow regional conventions. Likewise, layout conventions should conform to regional sensibilities, as should more subtle aspects such as the visual metaphors used in graphics, or the sorting order of text lists.

A straightforward way to support multiple regions is to use regional web sites to meet the needs of regional visitors. To present a consistent public presence globally, the regional sites should share common elements such as graphic design, application logic, look and feel, and navigation design. For example, a press release announcing the worldwide release of a product should have the same look-and-feel, but contain translated content in all regional sites. In contrast, an announcement of a product promotion launched as a tie-in to a national holiday season would be presented to a single region. As we'll see, it is a challenge to produce the many regional web sites efficiently, while avoiding duplicate efforts.

Globalizing a web site consists of two efforts: internationalize and localize. To *internationalize* a web site means to isolate region-specific content, such as text strings and time and date representation, from region-independent formatting and business logic. To *localize* a web site means to customize the region-specific content, also known as *resources*, to conform to expectations for a specific region. Separating the development effort into the dual efforts of internationalization and localization leads to the following principle:

> *Fundamental Principle of Globalization:*
> A core web development group maintains the internationalized web assets, while regional content contributors and developers create and modify localized assets.

The assets that comprise a web site need to be factored into region-dependent and region-independent parts. (See Figure 9.1.) In this way, the processes of developing and maintaining a web site share many of the characteristics of software development.

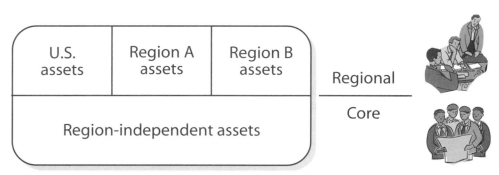

FIGURE 9.1
Effective globalization layers the region-specific assets on top of common region-independent assets.

The same is true for well-designed multi-platform software, which is factored into platform-dependent and platform-independent parts.

Certain aspects of web development should be controlled and managed by a core web team. Similarly, a product-focused software development organization typically employs a core development team to enable it to release a product on several operating system platforms simultaneously. Factoring the platform-independent code allows a core development team to make a single change and have it propagate to many platforms. In the same way, factoring the region-independent web assets allows a core web team to maintain a consistent look-and-feel, and allow it to deploy a single core change efficiently to many regions.

Establishing a core development group for common functions has benefits. Suppose the core development group decides to implement a common look-and-feel throughout the regional web sites with minimal disruption. Perhaps they want to introduce an updated color scheme for the corporate logo and related visual elements. Or perhaps they want to introduce a revamped navigation frame. By factoring the relevant assets into the core set, and by layering the region-specific assets on top, the regional web sites benefit from the shared management of common assets. This frees some time for the group to work on region-specific initiatives.

Careful thought should go into the agreement by which the core group and the regional group determine what constitutes a core asset and what constitutes a regional asset. For example, depending on the approach chosen, the top-level portal page could give tight control to the core development group, or could give wide autonomy to the regional group. The former gives better discipline over uniformity of look-and-feel and lets the regions run leaner operations. The latter gives the regions wider latitude to introduce new features and establish their unique identities.

This model of development allows wide latitude in the division of responsibilities between the core and the regional groups. Assigning the responsibility to the core group for such aspects as look-and-feel, templates, navigation, and so forth yields a high degree of uniformity among the regional web sites. Conversely, delegating a large amount of autonomy to the regional web sites by maintaining a minimal common core functionality grants wide discretion to the regional groups. The high-autonomy model can be effectively applied in a family of web sites that implement city-specific entertainment guides, for example. Each city would maintain a dedicated staff of web developers and content creators. The staff for the Los Angeles entertainment guide would be distinct from the staff for San Diego. At the same time, all the cities would share a common infrastructure group that maintains the event database and search engine.

A Globalization Initiative

In the remainder of this chapter we'll discuss how to design a web content management infrastructure for a fictitious suggestion provider, ezSuggestionBox.com. Let's assume that ezSuggestionBox.com has successfully rolled out its suggestion service to the U.S. and increasingly serves clients all over the world. The company decides to solidify its foothold outside the U.S. by globalizing its web property. So far, they haven't expended any effort to internationalize. Hence, the assets intertwine region-independent and region-specific content. For example, dates are hard-coded in the application engine to display in the U.S.-centric "mm/dd/yy" format. The user interface assumes U.S. English formatting conventions. These embedded assumptions must be located and repaired.

Here is the development game plan. See Figure 9.2. There are three phases. In the first phase, the web property exists and is maintained only in its original U.S.-only form. In the second phase, the globalization effort commences, while the original web

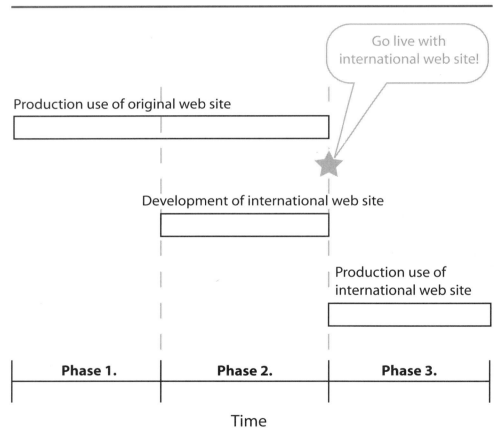

FIGURE 9.2

Development of the international web site proceeds in parallel with production use of the original web site.

site continues to be used in production. The effort creates an internationalized web property. Resource bundles hold assets for different locales. The completion of the internationalized web property marks the beginning of the third phase, when we cut over from the U.S.-only site to the internationalized site. Content changes propagate to multiple regional web sites. Changes to the internationalized web assets propagate to all regions, while changes made to region-specific resources propagate to the affected regions.

The assets that comprise the existing U.S.-only web site are shown in Figure 9.3. In this arrangement source code files written in a programming language such as Java or C++ encode the application logic. A build process produces several loadable modules that comprise the application engine. This runs within off-the-shelf applications servers that run on the production web servers. The web server renders additional assets consisting of images, HTML, and JavaScript. This is a common configuration.

The Easy Path Leads to Trouble

Gail starts a print job for the latest revision of her project schedule when she hears the rustling of papers and chairs as the managers' meeting disperses from the conference room around the corner. Rising from her chair, she wonders what had been decided about the international expansion of her company's web presence. Building a French regional web site seems to be the most logical step, she reasons to herself.

continued

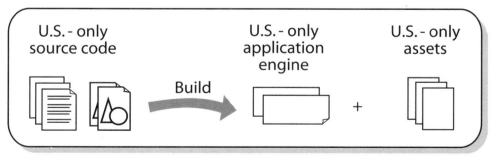

FIGURE 9.3
The existing U.S.-only web site has no separation of the region-independent and region-specific parts.

"Ah, there you are, Gail!" exclaims Gordon as he hurries toward her cube. Gordon is the director of web marketing. "I need your help," he explains. As he speaks, he imagines a web site hovering in front of him. His eyes intensely follow the form of his imaginary creation. His hands point to its contours. "We've gotten executive approval to build a French language web site. This is urgent. We've already lost three big deals because we're late translating our U.S. English web site into French. Just translate our English web site. That should work!"

Gail's mind races through alternatives. The web developers are already busy with two ambitious projects: an e-commerce initiative and a supply-chain integration effort. It is essential to keep those projects on track, while building the ability to handle French and German versions of their web site, followed by Chinese and Japanese in rapid succession. She calmly picks up a whiteboard marker.

"Here's how I think we should proceed," she explains to Gordon.

Before we introduce our preferred approach, we'll describe the approach advocated by Gordon, the fictitious web-marketing director—one that we might call the "wishful thinking" technique. Instead of factoring the various assets into region-independent and region-dependent parts to achieve the layering shown in Figure 9.1, we'll cut corners by creating a translated copy and hope for the best. Although we'll eventually learn that this path leads to failure, it is instructive to understand why this seemingly straightforward approach fails.

The approach of a one-time translation promises a quick win. The promise of an easy victory tempts us to take the shortest possible path: directly convert the assets and application engine to support another region. In other words, create an equivalent of the original U.S.-only web site, except translate it to serve another region. For example, Figure 9.4 shows an approach to converting the U.S.-only assets en masse for another locale, located in region A. This technique accomplishes its goal of converting the assets to suit another region without factoring the content and code into locale-independent and locale-dependent parts.

By eliminating this step of internationalizing, this technique leads to quicker completion. But there's a severe price paid for the short cut. Without the careful step of identifying the common locale-independent parts of the web assets from the locale-dependent parts, the immediate translation problem is solved, but it leaves bigger headaches.

Here's the first headache. Let's suppose the region A web site is a smashing success. Success implies taking the property to the next level, undertaking the next challenge. This implies continuing to enhance and maintain the content and the code for region A. Because we now have two separate and independent web sites, the work doubles. Each time someone changes the U.S. web site, that person or possibly someone else

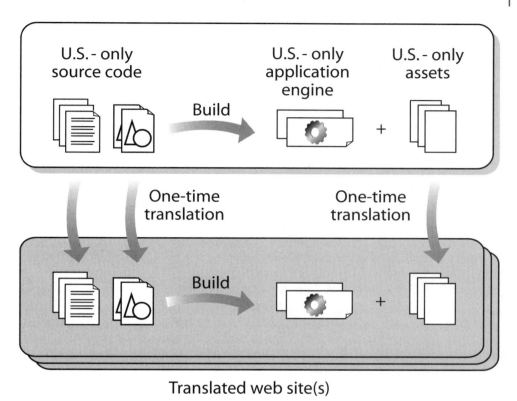

FIGURE 9.4
The one-time translation approach doesn't lend itself to common development across regions because it fails to factor out the common parts of the web sites.

needs to determine whether that change belongs in the region A web site as well. For some things, the answer will be obvious. For others, some investigation will yield the answer. Sometimes the answer is to make the same change. At other times, the answer is to make the equivalent translated change or culturally equivalent modification for the other locale. We've added the difficulty of determining how to propagate a change in one web site to the other web site.

Notice how we're beginning to fall down a slippery slope, because the work has more than doubled. In addition to making each change twice, there is the added effort to determine whether to make the change and how to effect the change. We've made our troubles much greater than they were originally, and we've become less efficient. Worse yet, with the increased workload, staffing needs to increase. The greater need to coordinate efforts ultimately imposes more frequent and more intricate communication between people working in related areas. Endless meetings and e-mails reduce efficiency, and we become less and less efficient as the evil-twin web site expands in size.

We've also introduced a second headache. What happens if we're asked to produce a web site for yet another region? We now have two candidates from which to copy. By now they've become different: less different if we've been scrupulously following our own procedures, more different if busy spells have caused us to omit procedures occasionally. With two copies of nearly everything, it becomes far less obvious to everyone involved which copy to prefer for reference purposes.

There's more bad news. There's a third source of headaches that promises to gnaw at everyone's long-term productivity. By building a fully replicated copy of everything for each region, we've built twice as many nooks and crannies for defects, bugs, and flaws to hide in. Defects love "dark places." A dark place is a line of code that executes infrequently. A dark place is an infrequently visited logic path or click sequence. A dark place is an image that users seldom see. By making a copy of everything, there are more dark places that are visited less frequently: more lines of code, more images, and more directories. There are more configuration files, where typos, errors of oversight, and faulty analyses hide. Defects will be harder to find and more plentiful.

All of the long-term headaches that we've highlighted originate from the initial questionable decision to gain a quicker payoff by copying the original U.S.-only web site and translating it. That approach produces troubles. Sometimes wishful thinking turns out to be just that.

Design a Solid Platform for International Development

The simplistic approach outlined in the previous section takes a path that ultimately leads to failure, but we can learn from the specific causes of the failure. Indeed, a fine distinction sometimes separates a simple approach from one that is simplistic. Hence we should pay our respects to the earlier solution, to analyze the causes of the breakdown. Let's summarize the deficiencies of the copy-and-translate approach:

1. Multiple copies of common code and assets lead to confusion.
2. Because required changes aren't isolated, it becomes cumbersome to later include additional regions.
3. Maintaining duplicate copies of assets is inefficient.

From these deficiencies, we see what's missing. There is no abstraction that separates what doesn't change during a translation effort, the common code, from that which endures the change, namely the region-specific assets. Without that separation, each successive translation effort bogs down from the sheer weight of the duplicated assets. From the first time the massive copy occurs there is an initial euphoric rush of superficial progress as the file count doubles. Deceptive, too, is the ease with which changes to the original web site continue to flow into the original. These quick initial wins evaporate.

Here lies the key to our puzzle. The copy-and-translate embodies the intense desire for a quick translation effort: get on with the task, and finish it. Without doubt, translation projects will tee up in rapid succession. They'll beg to be conducted in parallel.

Fixing the problem requires that we untangle two major aspects of the original web site. We lack an abstraction to distill content to be translated and localized from web assets that transcend specific regions. Externally, a web site has text and graphics that are visual, and internally it encodes logic that runs one or more aspects of a business operation. An important number of knowledge areas must be integrated, as shown in Table 9.1. They range from the high-level statement of the artistic and business intent, though the detailed embodiment of the user interface, the specific expressions of content, the various translations of the content into target language phrases, to the detailed manifestation of business and technical logic that runs the online presence. The wide range of knowledge represented in this list reflects the specialized skills realized in a web property.

Our solution should recognize the two different kinds of content, factoring the content according to the source of knowledge. This typically corresponds to the people that contribute to each. Although in this particular instance we're focusing on the translation aspect, the more general principle is that there are common factors that ought to be represented in one place, and there is the region-specific knowledge that is spread over many.

> *Factoring Principle:*
> Organize content to express each area of knowledge once.

TABLE 9.1
Sources of Knowledge that Comprise a Web Property.

Knowledge Area	Source of Knowledge
Look-and-feel.	Artistic design, business sponsor
Presentation of information (format and organization)	User interface design, graphic design
Original content	Content creation
Language and cultural context	Region-specific language skills and awareness of culture
Business logic, including personalization and programming	Business analysis, programming, information technology

Take the case of a press release for the worldwide release of a product. The core message should be expressed once, despite the fact that the headline, the short form, or the long form of the press release may be used in many different situations. At the same time, the U.S. Spanish version of the press release embodies distinct language-level translation and cultural knowledge, but expresses the same core message. Therefore, the translation wants to be expressed once, and then be made available for reuse.

The approach to structuring the assets follows the factoring pattern shown in Figure 9.5. The monolithic web assets are globalized by factoring the content into the part that is independent of the regions, separate from the region-specific assets.

Internationalize the assets and source code; this is the step that was skipped in the earlier solution. This effort pays off, because additional regions can be introduced with less overall effort, as shown in Figure 9.6 through the process of localization.

Here are some examples of differences in localized content. These examples illustrate subtleties of language and culture. Software developers and web developers need to be sensitive to these differences and strive to avoid embedding assumptions about sorting order, for instance, into the core logic of the web site.

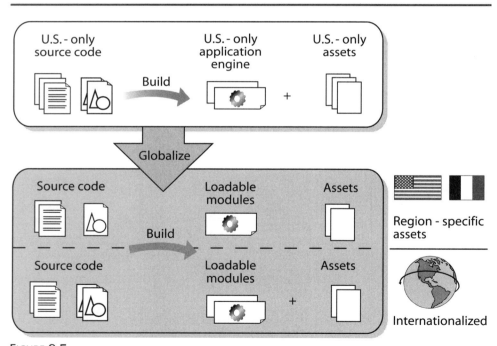

FIGURE 9.5

The primary thrust of the globalization project factors the web assets into the internationalized common parts and the region-specific parts.

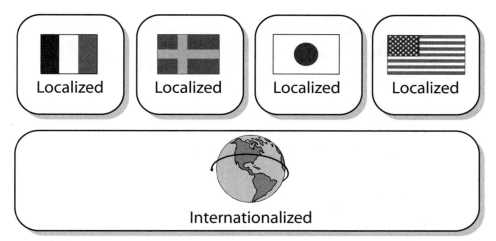

FIGURE 9.6
A globalized web site has an internationalized core that supports a set of localized assets for each region.

Date
Wednesday, April 4, 2001 (U.S.)
Mercredi, 4 avril 2001 (French)

Time
4:10 PM (U.S.)
16:10 (Japan)

Address
1195 West Fremont Ave., Sunnyvale, CA 94087 (U.S.)
Hibiya Central Bldg.13F, 1-2-9, Nishishinbashi, Munato-ku, Tokyo 105-0003 (Japan)

Telephone number
1 (408) 774-2000 (U.S.)
+81-3-5532-7000 (Japan)
+61 2 9657 1000 (Australia)

Sort order
A B C ... Z Å (Danish)
A B C Ç ... Z (French)

Branch Structure

Here are pertinent facts that guide how we structure the content:

a. We continue to manage the existing web site until we cut over to the international web site.

b. The internationalization effort splits the content into core and region-dependent parts.

c. Other regions are introduced as business needs dictate.

The branch structure shown in Figure 9.7 lets us run our globalization initiative in parallel with ongoing maintenance to the original web site. The branch structure allows the use of the original web site as the basis for continued operation of the business, while the internalization effort proceeds. To focus the effort we choose one specific region as the target. For example, a French translation shows that we can introduce abstractions that separate the core content from the U.S. English-specific content. A given section of the web site is internationalized by asking what constitutes the common part, and what constitutes the region-specific part.[1]

Here is how we derive the branch structure. First, identify the independent web sites. Clearly, the original web site and the need to maintain it during the conversion effort dictates that it be independent. It is a separate stream of work, and it deserves to be a separate branch.

Since the assets of the internationalized web site logically belong together, it constitutes a logically independent web site. The use of a single-branch model follows from the design guide. Therefore, the internationalized core portion of the web site together with the localized regional sites comprise a logically independent web site. Except for special situations that we'll consider shortly, there's no compelling reason to subdivide the content into branches.

Work Area Structure

The choice of the work area depends on how we expect the work to unfold. For example, if we foresee work proceeding as projects, we'd set up a per-project work area as shown in Figure 9.8. This arrangement would be especially appropriate for web site infrastructure changes made by the core group in the "common" directory structure.

---

[1] For example, the date renderer says, "December 3, 2000" in U.S. English, but for French it ought to say, "3 decembre 2000." In addition, time zone considerations imply that dates change at different times: 10 P.M. Eastern Standard Time on Monday is essentially Tuesday to most of the French-speaking world.

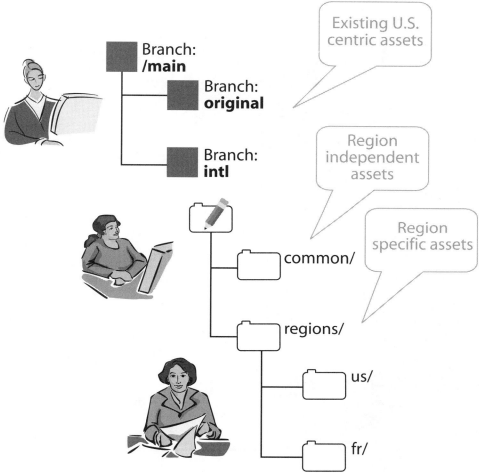

FIGURE 9.7
The original web site and the factored globalized web site are two logically independent web sites.

A per-time-slot work area structure as shown in Figure 9.9 might be appropriate for management of time-sensitive content. This situation could be especially applicable for the regional web sites.

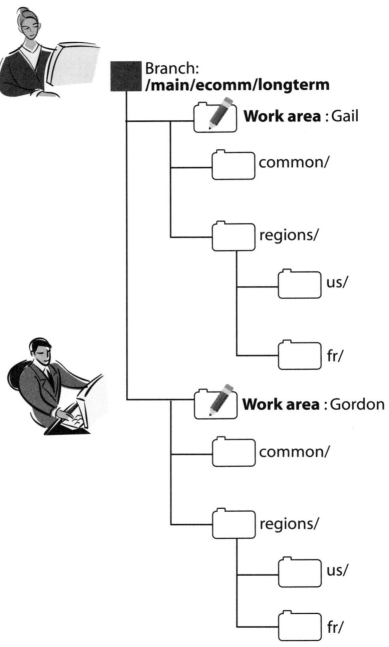

FIGURE 9.8
Separate work areas on the international branch let tasks proceed independently.

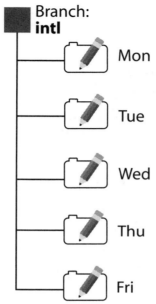

FIGURE 9.9
A per-time-slot work area structure orchestrates the movement of time-sensitive content to regional web sites.

Special Situations

If the number of assets exceeds a certain threshold that would make compute-intensive content management operations on the branch objectionable, this would warrant a further decomposition into subbranches. In this situation, the design of Figure 9.10 can be used.

The presence of a dual time situation is another reason to subdivide the international web site further into a separate branch for the short-term work, and another branch for the long-term work. This is shown in Figure 9.11.

Workflow Design

In this section, we'll propose a workflow design for the two-branch structure introduced earlier. The interaction sequences, especially those that cross organization or geographic boundaries, stand to benefit the most from codification as a formal workflow. Interactions occur frequently because translation involves many separate steps, and the think-time tends to be much less than the time that is spent waiting for the next person in the process to pick up the task. A workflow that assists the translation process will likely reap the greatest payback to the organization. In particular, we

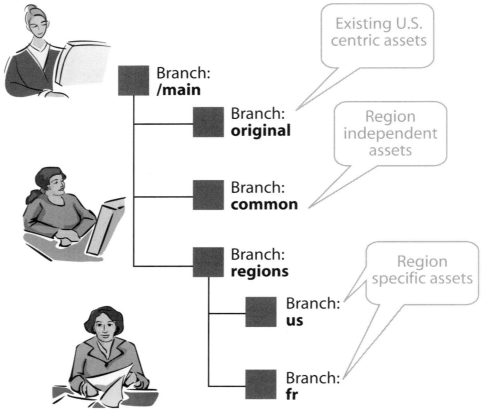

FIGURE 9.10
Do additional decomposition into branches if the number of assets on a single branch becomes unmanageable.

want to use workflow to minimize the wait-time involved in issuing and tracking work assignments for translation tasks, and to lessen the delays in getting necessary review and approvals of the completed work.

We'll focus now on a workflow to facilitate the translation process during the introduction of a new region and during ongoing operation of the web site. There are three job functions: editors, translators, and reviewers. An editor identifies the page or pages to be routed for translation. She chooses the target language, and assigns it to the group responsible for that language. When an assignment occurs, e-mail is sent to members of the group. The e-mail contains links to target pages. When a member of the group accepts the job, the files are updated into a designated work area. A work area is allocated from a pool of available work areas. When the work is done, the

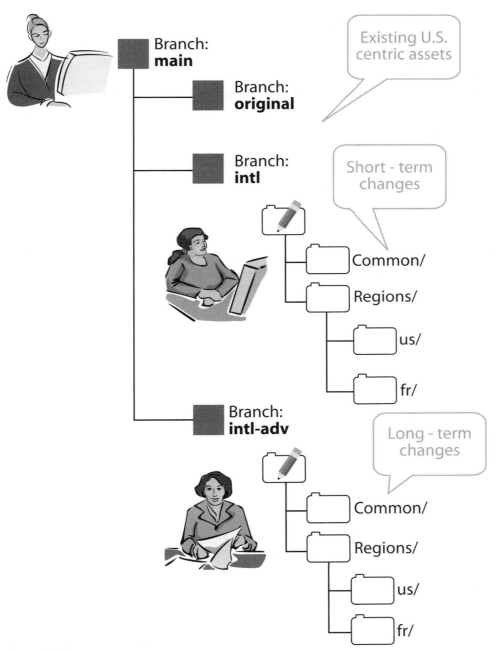

FIGURE 9.11
The long-term/short-term branch pattern separates long-term work from short-term work.

translator indicates completion, which offers the work to be checked by a group of reviewers. An e-mail to the potential reviewers contains links to the completed files. When a reviewer accepts the task, it becomes his or hers. The reviewer studies the completed files in the context of a working web site, and either renders an approval (which pushes the task to the next state), or sends the task back to the group or to the original translator for rework. On approval, the files are submitted to the staging area, a notification e-mail is automatically generated, and the task is logged to a database. Files that could not be submitted because of conflicts are flagged, and an e-mail is generated. A means is provided to initiate another task to resolve the conflicts easily. Figure 9.12 shows the translation process workflow. The many interactions in the translation and review process are diagrammed in Figure 9.13.

Template System Design

Translation lends itself naturally to the use of a template subsystem to capture structured content. Tagged text captured in the language of the original is of a particular structure—a press release, a product description, a frequently asked question, a list of product features and benefits, or technical support advice. The content acquires additional tags to indicate the language, the creator, the creation time, keywords, index categories, information on whether it should be routed for translation, and an expiration date

Figure 9.14 shows how a template system captures structured input, and how workflow routes content for further processing. In this case, translators working off-site receive task routings and hand off completed work for review. A data content record holds both the translated information for each product, along with metadata such as the date that the product goes live. In the example shown in Figure 9.14, we see that the French-speaking region uses a different effective date. This illustrates how culture, language, and other factors impact globalization.

Deployment Design

Because of the separation between the internationalized core content and the localized regional content, each regional web site is built much like software. The built assets are submitted to the staging area, and published into editions. From that point, there are deployment units to move the content to specific regional web servers. For example, the French regional web server farm receives a deployment of the built core plus French assets.

The deployment design presented here could be used for either the original site or the internationalized site. This is a typical deployment design that is suitable for a medium-size web team, say, 20 developers and QA engineers. For a team of this size, it is common for a half-dozen projects to be running simultaneously. No single person can stay on top of all pending changes. At the same time, business needs require that changes move quickly and precisely to the production web site. This is where the

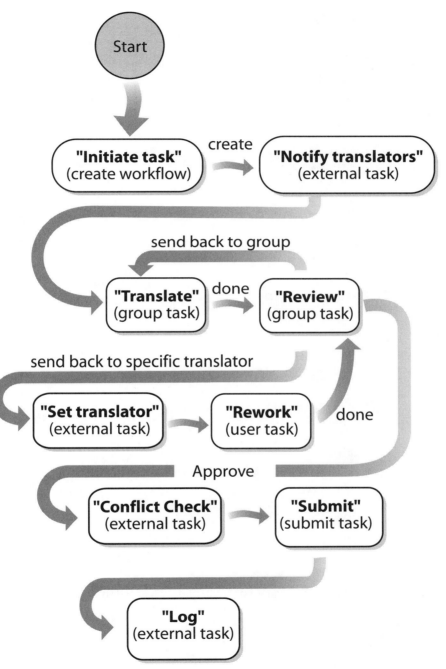

FIGURE 9.12
Translation process workflow moves content through the approval and submit processes.

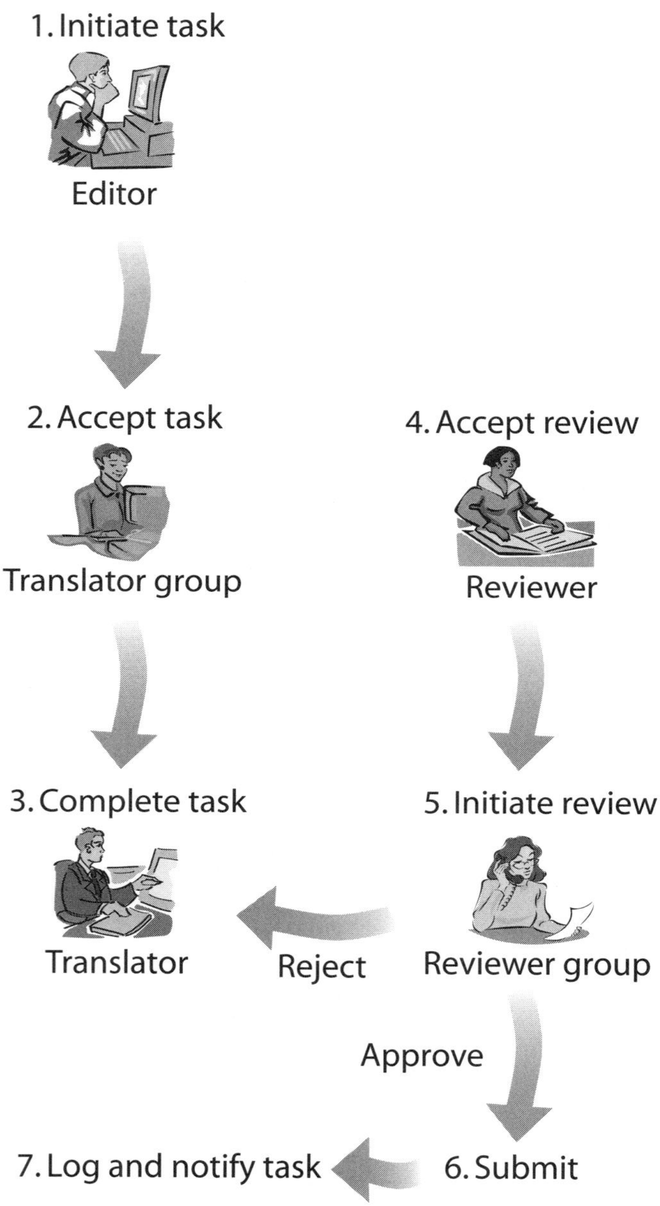

1. Initiate task

Editor

2. Accept task

Translator group

4. Accept review

Reviewer

3. Complete task

Translator   Reject

5. Initiate review

Reviewer group

Approve

7. Log and notify task   6. Submit

FIGURE 9.13
The translation and review workflow involves many interactions.

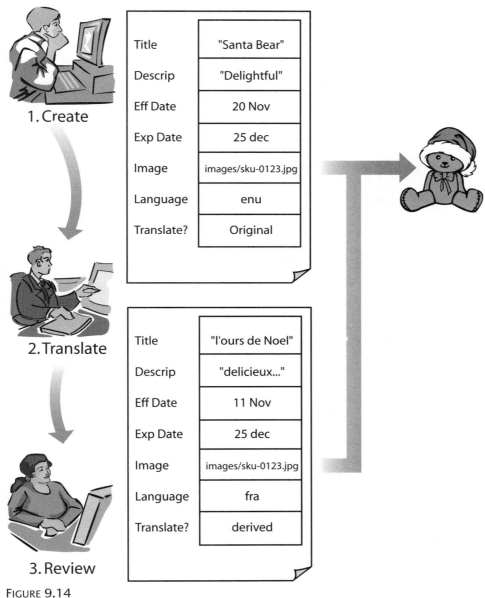

FIGURE 9.14
Templates facilitate the creation and translation of localized resources.

deployment infrastructure comes in. We'll assume that changes to be deployed from the production side have been approved and submitted. These follow the release agreement described in Chapter 7. For instance, changes may be tracked through a workflow mechanism. For our purposes, by the time changes are handled by the deployment system, assets have been reviewed, approved, and placed under version control in an appropriate manner.

Figure 9.15 shows a deployment infrastructure that uses a single production server. The deployment design satisfies the following requirements:

1. Allows most changes to be moved into production during off-peak hours.
2. Supports the ability for a web producer to move specific, urgent files and directory changes to production on-demand.
3. Supports the ability to roll back the production web site to a designated known-good version.
4. Takes periodic snapshots of the staging area—daily, for example—to serve as known-good rollback versions.

As shown in Table 9.2, three deployment units comprise the deployment infrastructure: scheduled, immediate, and rollback.

Summary

We've shown how a web property can apply the techniques of web content management to build an infrastructure to support a globalization initiative. We introduced a branch structure to reflect the two major initiatives, one to continue development and maintenance of the original U.S.-centric web site, and the other to factor the web assets into a common internationalized subset. Localized assets embody the region-specific aspects of the site. We used a template system to facilitate creating and editing structured content, including translated content. We used a workflow subsystem to boost efficiency by minimizing wait-time and facilitating multiple step translation processes. Finally, we designed a deployment system to move completed web assets to the regional destinations reliably and efficiently.

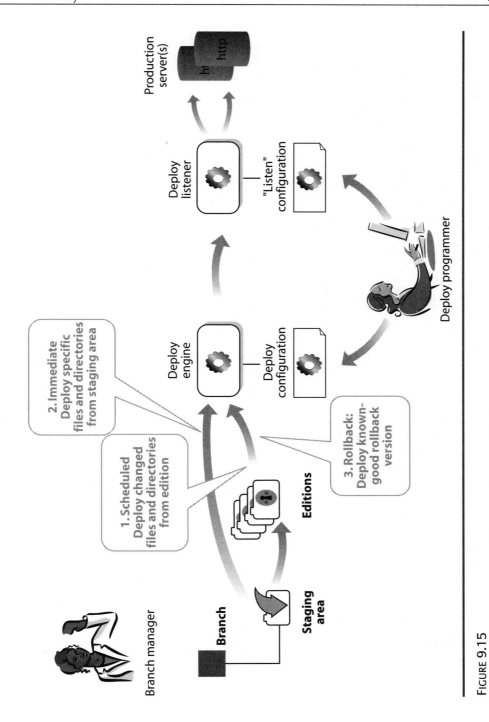

FIGURE 9.15
This deployment infrastructure uses a single production server.

TABLE 9.2
Basic Deployment Units for a Medium-size Web Operation

Name	Description	What is Deployed	When Initiated	Who Initiates	Deploy Mode	Script Intergration
1. Scheduled	Move normal changes to production server, according to schedule.	All changes in staging area	According to schedule	Automatic job	Comparison-driven, positive and negative changes.	Before and after deploy, scripts cycle web server. Notification on success and failure.
2. Immediate	Move urgent changes to production server as soon as possible.	Files and directories on change list	On-demand	Web producer, via user interface	List-driven, positive changes. Transactional.	Before and after deploy, scripts cycle web server. Notification on success and failure.
3. Rollback	Roll back the production web site to a predetermined known-good version. Support rollback by defining the rollback versions regularly.	Rollback version, typically all of a particular edition	On-demand	Production manager, via user interface	Comparison-driven, positive and negative changes. Transactional.	Before and after deploy, scripts cycle web server. Notification on success and failure.

CHAPTER TEN

SUMMARY AND CONCLUSIONS

The philosophy of one century is the common sense of the next.

—*Henry Ward Beecher*

Executive Summary

We revisit the five rules introduced in Chapter 1. The rules remind us to focus on our assets, to adopt an iterative approach to development, to be responsive to customers, to make it easy for content contributors to create and modify assets, and to build a manageable and reproducible infrastructure. These imperatives challenge us to organize web development activities for efficiency and responsiveness. Core challenges include the following:

- Instituting versioning
- Managing concurrency
- Managing project completion skew
- Building a manageable deployment infrastructure
- Exploiting workflow to compress work cycles
- Separating long-term from short-term changes
- Introducing simple interfaces for content contributors
- Accommodating very large web sites

The content management solutions all rely on four subsystems. First, a content repository subsystem provides versioning and configuration management services. Second, a creation and editing environment makes it easy for content developers. Third, a workflow and job routing subsystem boosts efficiency and reduces wait-time. Finally, a deployment subsystem reliably copies content to production and fosters a clear separation between development and production.

Each subsystem has a distinct and useful function. As we examine the ways that each subsystem is called upon to do more or to integrate more tightly with other subsystems, it becomes readily apparent that each can be considerably expanded. We examine each of the four subsystems. By observing usage pattern trends, we suggest how these subsystems will expand their capabilities in the future.

Introduction

Content management continues to change and adapt. Some changes originate from external pressures of the customers of information technology, such as consumers, businesses, and clients from within an organization. Other changes originate from technological innovations, such as web servers, or application servers, and the like. As content management incorporates innovations from areas of server technology, network infrastructure, and browser technologies, its capabilities will doubtlessly expand. These changes reinforce one other. The ability to integrate traditional back-end services, such as order status tracking, with a 24×7 customer-facing self-service web front-end alters the equilibrium. These changes generate forces within the foundational structures of information technology that promise more and cause clients to expect more. As customers come to expect more, more is expected from the information technology staff. Business expands. Customers are happier.

But amidst this change comes a growing recognition that content drives business, and hence content drives the concepts and methodologies that we use to think about the business. The phrases "web content management" and "web production" have recent origins. They attempt to capture the importance of focusing attention on the content flowing through a web infrastructure and the processes used to manage the production operation. There are four major subsystems of content management infrastructure (Figure 10.1). This book explains how to conceptualize the problems that web teams face; it attempts to give a sense of the everyday struggle to cope with the forces building within the practices, tools, and concepts of information technology.

Revisiting the Rules

Let's revisit the rules that we introduced in the first chapter. Earlier these rules helped us to understand the forces that have transformed the running of a business because of the opportunities and pressures afforded by the Internet. The rules underscored

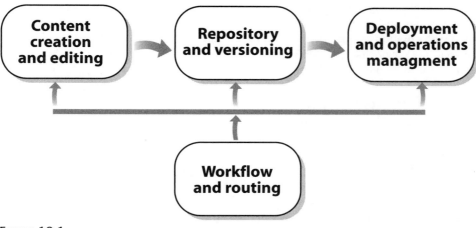

FIGURE 10.1
Four major subsystems of content management infrastructure.

the importance of content management in comparison with informal techniques. We now look at the rules from a different perspective. With a firm grasp of the principles of content management, our perspective of the rules shifts to the next level of sophistication.

It's the Assets, Stupid!

Assets continue to play a pivotal role. With assets safely versioned and stored in a repository, the focus shifts to broader kinds of assets and the way that we manage them. We separate (factor) content from presentation. We factor the regional content from the core internationalized web property. We automate important aspects of the management of our assets, including their deployment and replication. And we improve our ability to manage assets by introducing the concept of metadata. *Metadata* is information about a particular asset; typically it consists of brief descriptive tags describing the asset owner, creation date, expiration date, index keywords, and so forth. Tagging assets with metadata enhances our ability to search, reuse, and expire our assets effectively.

The presence of assets tagged with metadata encourages automated processing of assets, including indexing, searching, expiration, and deploying. Processing takes the form of hand-coded scripts and configuration files. These files encode knowledge about how we manage our assets. Note that we've come full circle. These configuration and script files are themselves valuable assets that need to be managed! We have new assets that describe how to manage other assets. How should we treat them? The solution is clear. Treat each asset as an entity to be managed in our repository. Details of how a business runs are valuable assets. These include content that a customer views, information about when and how a piece of content should be viewed (i.e., metadata), a script that specifies how the production server should prepare to receive a deployment, or a lowly configuration file.

Experiment. Iterate. Grow.

Iteration is the key. Plan to have the shortest possible time between meaningful releases of software or between checkpoints of a web property. Whenever there's a set of deliverables, ask whether they can be divided and delivered separately, sequentially, or in parallel. Gone are the days of the gargantuan release that tries to do it all. If you have a small deliverable and a big deliverable, and they can be deployed separately, try to do so. You'll be surprised how often, when the smaller deliverable goes first, you'll learn much more about how it is received by customers, what it takes to maintain the feature. New ideas spring from the previous deliverable, and show how to improve it on the next iteration. Compare where you would have been had you not decoupled the deliverables. Chances are that you will find that the fielding of the first idea significantly alters your priorities. You might even learn that the second idea needs to be substantially changed, or that a second iteration of the first deliverable should take precedence over the second deliverable. Learning comes from an iterative dialogue with your customers, suppliers, and partners.

Respond to Customers Quickly and Frequently, or Lose Them!

Opportunities are perishable. There is a limited window of opportunity to remedy a deficiency or to introduce an innovation. Rendering a product or service can be thought of as having a dialog with the recipient. The ongoing dialog includes responding to customer feedback. Even a partial, imperfect response communicates empathy, and above all, a willingness to listen. That goes a long way to fostering more interactions and opening an avenue for further pleas for help. In this light, a steady stream of complaints and suggestions can be viewed as a positive: a sequence of invitations to engage in a conversation. Responding quickly and frequently keeps the conversation going. Use the efficiency improvements offered by workflow, branching for multiple initiatives, and a deployment subsystem to speed changes and improvements to customers. Respond quickly by iterating early and often.

There's an important role for asset tagging in responding quickly. Asset tags in the form of metadata help drive personalization systems, which reach focused subsets of customer groups more readily.

Enable the Masses!

The history of computing and information technology in general has been accompanied by an ongoing trend to demystify, simplify, and increase access to previously impenetrable and lofty technology. In the context of content management, demystification means making it easier for more people inside and outside an organization to contribute. Contributions might come from in-house content specialists such as marketers and technical support representatives, or outside vendors, or customers, suppliers, and partners. Each person is a specialist within his or her job description. Weaving them into the fabric of the larger organization entails finding ways to accept their input and to present information to them in meaningful ways. Invest in the content creation and editing subsystems to leverage their expertise.

Content originates from many sources, including other information systems such as syndication, business-to-business, and supply-chain integration systems. If these systems are integrated into the web content infrastructure, the synergy benefits the entire organization. In effect, all the contributors that directly or indirectly add their content to the other systems augment the whole. For example, when a retailer's web operation integrates product catalog content syndicated directly from manufacturers or from information resellers, the outside sources effectively enlarge the pool of contributors. Enable the masses, inside and out.

Make It Manageable and Reproducible

The Internet stitches groups and departments together as never before. In the past, the Internet frontier represented untamed badlands and was the province of renegades and misfits. After the early pioneers tamed the wilderness of Internet technologies, they brought new capabilities to the citizens of the larger corporate commonwealth. Here are some guidelines for this new territory. First, running a modern Internet operation requires doing the right thing. Second, make it repeatable and reliable. Get it right once, and then figure out how to make it happen reliably. You can use a creation and editing environment to rapidly iterate to get it right, then use the repository to put the assets under version control. Then, use workflow and notification techniques to keep people abreast of changes. Use deployment to move changes into production.

Future Trends

Each of the functional building blocks described earlier has a distinct purpose within the system. When we examine those functions within the context of rapidly evolving and demanding business environments, some basic trends become apparent. One trend is that the best possible implementation of a particular subsystem available today will pale in comparison to what it might become in the near future with continued evolution, refinement, and specialization. This implies that we improve the ability of a subsystem to execute its function within the context of the whole. Another trend is that content will continue to play an integral role in the operation of a business, focusing the spotlight on the processes and practices that become necessary for such integration. Here are more details about the major trends.

Content Becomes More Structured

Structured data means packaging a more complex data element out of basic data types, augmenting a data element by associating metadata with it, or by doing both.[1] Take the example of a video clip intended for delivery over the web. By itself, it satisfies its objective of delivering its content to the end user. Its usefulness is greatly enhanced by combining it with additional information, such as a title, a short description, a summary of the contents, and perhaps a transcript of the audio portion of the video. The video clip could be rendered in a variety of resolutions to suit different bandwidth requirements. Add metadata, or data about the data itself. Add keywords to facilitate indexing and search, including the duration of the video clip, the creation date, the creator, the release date, an identifier code that uniquely identifies that video clip, and perhaps an expiration date. Because the data is structured, component parts of the data can be accessed and used separately. This promotes reuse. The flexibility of being able to select the parts that are relevant to an intended purpose encourages multiple uses. For example, the low-bandwidth video clip, together with the title and the short description can be repackaged for free distribution, while the full suite of bandwidth compatible clips could be distributed or syndicated on a payment basis.

Files and databases continue to be used heavily. This is just the beginning of their use because any composite data element such as the video clip example will be assembled incrementally by many specialists. Review, approval, and versioning actions on the asset themselves create additional metadata. Again we've come full circle.

Structured content imposes additional demands on the content repository to store, index, and retrieve content completely or in part, according to the particular structure. In addition, structures will change, causing us to revise an older structure to coexist with newer content with a different, compatible structure.

Content Contributors and Their Tools Become More Specialized

As the web matures we find that the diversity of the applications increases and the data types become more varied. Information technology managers face an explosion in the variety of tools. There's a need for even more specialized tools to cope with a

---

[1] XML is a popular representational format for structured data.

wider range of contributors and data that are more varied.[2] Workers that assist or review content suddenly become contributors. For example, suppose a video clip like the one described in the previous section undergoes a legal, artistic, or technical review step. The fact that the review step has occurred, together with information about who did the review, when it occurred, along with commentary, becomes an integral part of the data package. In the realm of content distribution, assets transformed for wide-scale distribution have many formats of audio and video, in both downloadable and streaming form. In the entertainment industry alone, the profusion of digital formats, the growing magnitude of piracy, and the hectic rethinking of business models reflects the turmoil in that segment.[3,4,5] These forces will inevitably intrude on the content creators and related specialists. For example, adoption of digitally signed or watermarked[6] assets types to augment copyright protection will lead to new processes and tools. With more specialization, we want a wide selection of tools suited to each specific application. We can predict pressures for tools to follow uniform tagging conventions and for standards governing interoperability with a tag-aware content repository.

Blurring the Distinction between Web Operations and the Rest of Business

Without doubt, web technologies will continue to diffuse into mainstream business operations, fostering tighter integration across boundaries that traditionally separate vendors, suppliers, and partners. Just as no one distinguishes the "computer-enabled" side of their business from the "non-computer-enabled," a continuation of the trend toward diffusion of boundaries means that web operations will become indistinguishable from the rest of the business. For example, when a technical support group maintains a support web site in addition to running a traditional telephone-based operation, the two support channels simply become different ways of reaching the customer base. The web merely becomes a new option for support. It ceases to become a novel or experimental course of action, but instead it becomes part of the business fabric. This incorporation into the business fabric has important implications

---

[2] Byron Bignell and William Rogers, "Simplifying web content management underestimated as e-business challenge," Sun Server, August 2000. See also http://www.sunservermagazine.com/sun0800/content.htm.

[3] Connie Ling, "Asia's entertainment industries fight to cope with VCD piracy," *The Wall Street Journal Interactive Edition*, March 29, 1999.

[4] Nathan Beckord, "Revolution," New Investment Frontiers, May 26, 2000. See also http://ragingbull.lycos.com/cgi-bin/static.cgi/a=05-26-00.txt&d=articles/beckord.

[5] Charles Cooper, "Entertainment execs: learning to live with piracy," ZDNet Interactive Week, August 3, 2000.

[6] Stefan Katzenbeisser and Fabien A. P. Petitcolas, eds., *Information Hiding Techniques for Steganography and Digital Watermarking*, Artech House Books, 1999.

for the discipline of web content management. No longer a curiosity, content creation and editing tools will be diffused throughout an organization; and they will be expected to function effectively, to do so dependably, and be easy to use.

More Distributed and Flow-based Handling of Assets, Tasks, and Jobs

Because an ever-widening circle of participants create and maintain a given asset, two realities enter the picture. First, the circle of participants is more likely to encompass contributors outside the immediate organization. Examples include a firm specializing in graphic design, an outside law firm reviewing legal documents, and a web design agency building a new section of a web property. Second, the wider circle of contributors necessarily implies more frequent handoffs and shorter work cycles. By slicing a work process into basic unit tasks assigned to the most capable specialist and by bringing relevant resources to bear on the problem, the overall quality rises. The challenge shifts to building a workflow infrastructure to "flow" the tasks among the virtual teams, while minimizing handoff delays.

The use of syndicated content illustrates the benefits of distributed, flow-based handling of assets. The content itself includes news stories, product catalog information, or units of product support information; however, the flow of management information about the content is likely to represent many times the volume of the primary information. Each piece of content has a lifecycle that undergoes creation and delivery phases. The creation phase of its lifecycle entails numerous discrete management steps, including assignment, notification, review, approval, all multiplied by the number of iterations required to complete the content. The content itself transitions through a handful of work stages, while the information flow associated with the overall management is considerably larger. Similarly, during the delivery phase of the lifecycle, the delivery itself consists of relatively straightforward data transfer, while the information flow associated with the management overhead is larger. The content provider generates, indexes, and promulgates information about the content itself, while the content accessor searches, queries, fetches, and samples potential candidates. Once a decision has been made, the accessor solicits, purchases, receives, and acknowledges the chosen item. After delivery, the content provider monitors usage, gathers feedback, and requests payment for the content. A distributed, flow-based handling of assets makes this possible.

It should be no great surprise that transaction flow to manage the creation and delivery of content typically outstrips the transfer of the content itself, because exactly the same phenomenon occurs for goods in the physical world. As the flow of assets increases across departments within a business or between companies, the activities to manage the flow will evolve to mirror the information transmittals accompanying physical goods. We conclude that the pace, frequency, and level of automation will rise substantially for information-based content.

More Emphasis on Content Tagging to Enable Storage, Retrieval, Search, Reuse, and Routing

Content reuse and syndication open new means to extract additional economic value from the inherent worth of an asset, such as text, graphics, and rich media types. In a conventional web site, an asset lives its existence embedded within an HTML page. Reuse is possible, but it requires that the asset be tagged with information about the asset itself, a tag sometimes referred to as *metadata*. It will carry basic information such as its description, its creator, and its creation date, together with indexing information, usage guidelines, and related information. In some ways the tagging of an asset, whether primitive data type or a composite, is no different from a composite data type of which a subset is the metadata. To be freely mobile in its own right, an asset will carry descriptive metadata, which serve as credentials. Eventually, it will acquire an identity of its own. Content tagging requires a tag-savvy repository.

Today we stand at the beginning of an explosion of content, both in raw quantity and in terms of richness of types. As the quantity and richness of content expand, the need to apply and manage metadata will shift from something optional, to an absolute requirement. In the familiar physical world, an object becomes unusable for two possible reasons. The object is destroyed, or the object is misplaced. For example, a pair of sunglasses cannot be used when we need them either because they have been destroyed, or because they have been mislaid. Unlikely to have been destroyed, the sunglasses are sitting in one of a number of obvious locations, but we're not sure which one. Our problem becomes magnified as the quantity and value of our belongings increase, and there are more things and more places in which to misplace them. As we create greater quantities of truly useful content, our success hinges critically on our ability to tag, index, store, search, access, retrieve, use, and reuse the content.

Emphasize 24 x 7 Management Infrastructure

The need for 24 × 7 uptime to most organizations is abundantly clear. A business-to-consumer operation (B2C) cannot assume that consumers cease to visit a web property at any particular time of day, or day of the week. This is especially true for global operations. Two o'clock Sunday morning in Boston might seem like a good time to schedule server downtime and maintenance, but that's prime Monday afternoon for Far East staffers working in Sydney, Australia. The ever-widening reach of global business operations, coupled with the expectation of universal connectivity severely constrains management options. A business-to-business (B2B) operation faces many of the same constraints. Business considerations drive the scheduling of catalog updates and information interchange between business partners and take precedence over mere convenience. Even though a supplier of updated product images falls behind schedule, the online catalog operator must complete the integration with revised price information by the appointed deadline. There's little tolerance for downtime, scheduled or unscheduled. Indeed, there will be a continued shift from reactive responses to downtime, to proactive management of uptime. To alert administrator personnel when a content deployment fails due to storage-full conditions in the server farm is commendable. To have detected in advance that the scheduled deployment event would exhaust the storage capacity on the production servers is even better.

In reactive mode, a heroic effort by the system administration crew achieves corrective action in, say, one hour, instead of several hours if the monitoring system weren't in place. In proactive mode, the system administration staff expands storage capacity in routine fashion, and there is no downtime at all. The shift in mode can be imperceptible but requires a mind-shift on the part of management. The avoidance of last-minute heroics should itself be deemed heroic. Wise managers cheer the uneventful handling of business challenges as much as they do a showy display of valor. The path to success builds on a 24 × 7 proactive management infrastructure.

Conclusion

As we've seen, the four fundamental parts of a web content management system include a repository, a contributor-friendly editing environment, a workflow subsystem, and a deployment subsystem. We've identified concepts and principles that help us exploit content management to achieve business goals. Many of the principles define a healthy social fabric that binds an effective web operation. In small development organizations, peer pressure encourages members, for example, to scrupulously adhere to testing and review guidelines on all submitted assets. Larger organizations achieve the same end through greater reliance on formal procedures enforced by explicit workflow steps, despite the normal inflow of new members and their divergent backgrounds. Use your judgment to determine when to lean toward informality and simplicity, and when more formal structures and procedures are warranted. Balance the benefits that derive from greater standardization against the inevitable inflexibility that rigid procedures confer on the organization.

As you go forward to design and implement a content management infrastructure, keep in mind that your most important assets are the people that comprise the organization and the skills that they bring with them. In addition to the people, time is another precious asset. Make effective use of time and effort, for example, by using techniques that empower developers to move rapidly knowing that version-controlled assets reside safely in the repository. Use notification within workflow to eliminate idle time within task handoffs. Arrange tools and infrastructure to efficiently gather structured content through the use of data capture forms, and to economically express look-and-feel decisions within a common presentation template.

Web content management plays a vital role in the smooth functioning of a business-critical web operation. You can build a robust content management infrastructure by combining good tools, common sense, and the concepts and principles that we've covered in this book.

Part Four

APPENDICES

APPENDIX A

A SMART FILE SYSTEM

A smart versioning file system gives developers multiple independent copies of web assets corresponding to a web site. It simultaneously manages the underlying storage so that unmodified copies of a given file appearing in many work areas are stored only once. We'll refer to this as a *smart file system*.

Figure A.1 shows that the smart file system contains files that are themselves stored in a physical medium, which we call a *backing store*. The files in a work area are stored in the backing store. The smart file system keeps track of when a file is unmodified or modified, to minimize the number of distinct files stored in the backing store.

As shown in Figure A.2, when a file is modified, it is saved in the backing store.

Let's see how this approach scales to many developers. In Figure A.3, we see how each developer uses a separate copy of the web site. Each copy of the web site assets resides in a directory structure denoted in the figure by a folder icon.

For example, a typical large-scale web site might consist of 100,000 files consuming 5 GB of storage. A plain file system stores 5 GB of storage for each developer. If we have 10 developers who each need a separate copy of the web site, and we store the files in a plain file system, then we need 50 GB. This is wasteful because each developer typically changes a relatively small number of files, compared to the web site as a whole.

The essential point is that a smart file system arranges to keep a single copy of unmodified files, across all the web site copies in the work areas. Because a smart file system lets client workstations mount different work areas across a network, developers work in the same way as if the files were stored locally on their workstations.

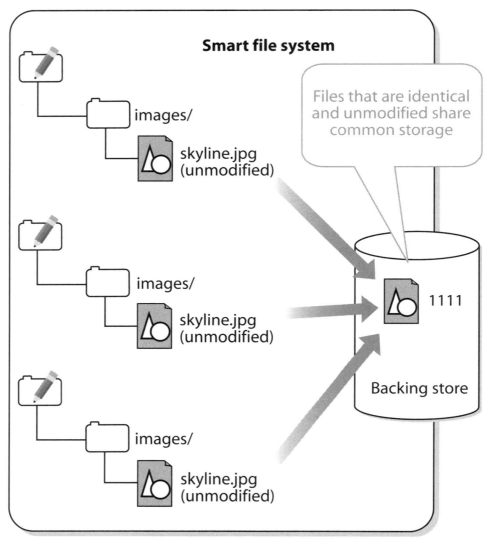

FIGURE A.1
Another work area containing unmodified files doesn't consume additional space in the backing store.

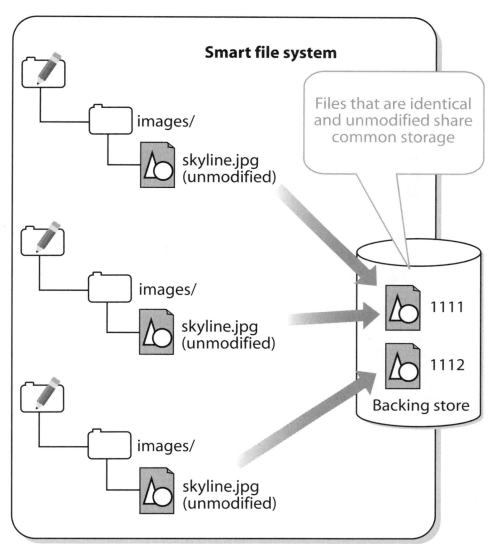

FIGURE A.2
Modifying a file uses additional storage.

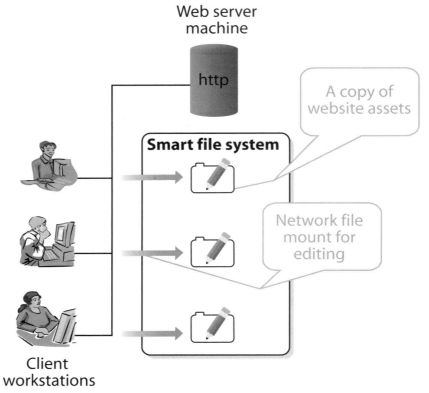

FIGURE A.3
A smart file system supports many developers.

It is a straightforward task to configure a content editing tool to work in a smart file system. The same principles outlined earlier apply here as well:

1. The client workstation mounts the disk volume of the smart file system.
2. On each client workstation, the editing tool is pointed at the location of the root of the web site for the developer.
3. The user of the tool uses relative references and absolute references.

A WORKFLOW DESIGN FOR FORMAL HAND OFF BETWEEN GROUPS

Executive Summary

A common organizational arrangement for web development enforces a formal transfer process to move content from development to testing. For example, web content developers hand off new and modified web assets to a quality assurance (QA) group. The separation provides a buffer between a fast-paced, free-wheeling content development group and a rigorous QA group. The QA group evaluates a fixed snapshot of the proposed changes. A QA engineer tests the changes based on the snapshot and makes a formal determination of approval or of rejection. On approval, the changes are submitted and prepared for production. On rejection, the original developer is notified, and after more changes, the cycle starts over again. This appendix describes a workflow specification that supports the formal hand-off paradigm.

Introduction

Sandy enjoyed her new responsibility as quality assurance lead for the eportalzone.com portal web site. Although she joined the team as a web developer, she found greater satisfaction scrutinizing changes from the other web developers before the changes went live. Meanwhile, Rick's web development team had grown to ten developers, and the posting of

continued

new content to their portal web site had become a continuous barrage of changes. Over time, Sandy's quality assurance team has expanded into a full-time team of four quality assurance specialists juggling scores of changes daily. Sandy finds that a strong predictor of success and enjoyment in the role of QA specialist is an interest in details and an inquisitive personality.

As a web operation grows, roles of the team members become increasingly specialized. In a small operation, a developer might shepherd a change all the way from concept, to implementation, to approval, to testing, to moving the change into production. As the team grows larger, it is common for the content development and quality assurance roles to be more sharply delineated. A typical way to enforce this separation of the roles is to introduce a hand-off step between groups. By *hand-off step*, we mean a distinct step where an identified collection of new and modified files, or *change set*, is presented to a quality assurance (QA) group for testing and approval. At the time the hand off occurs, reference copies of the files contained in the change set are made, which allows QA to have unchanging content to test.

Requirements

We describe the formal hand-off paradigm as follows. First, there is an explicit hand off between development and QA. Second, changes in the developer's work area are captured at the time that the hand off occurs. Third, the assignment of a QA person to take responsibility for a change set isn't known in advance, but instead this occurs after the hand off. Fourth, each QA person has one or more preferred testing areas, to which the changes are propagated after they take ownership of a given change set. Fifth, changes may be submitted to the staging area only after they have been through QA testing and approval.

These requirements lead to the design presented here. The requirement that submission of changes to staging may only occur subsequent to testing and approval by QA and the need to snapshot the changes imply that there be some kind of holding area for the changed content. The original work area of the developer cannot be used, because this doesn't provide a formal hand-off point. For example, this opens the door for additional changes to be sneaked into the change list, thereby violating the formal hand-off paradigm. Because the untested and unapproved changes cannot be submitted to staging, additional work areas are necessary.

QA Hand-off Workflow

The logic of the hand-off workflow is shown in Figure B.1. A developer makes changes. When the changes are complete, they are handed off to the QA group. A member of the QA group tests the changes, and either approves or rejects the changes. If the changes are approved, the changes proceed through a release process.

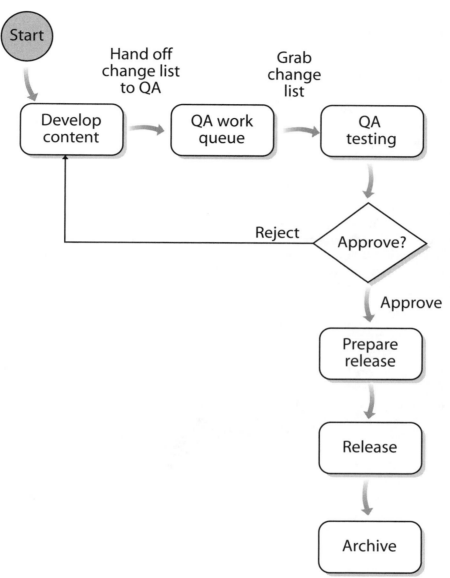

FIGURE B.1
The QA hand-off workflow uses a formal hand-off step.

Figure B.2. presents another view of the process. It shows the movement of the change list as it transitions from development, through testing, to submit. Developer work areas are shown on the left, each holding the change set for a single task.[1] When the task is complete, the developer hands off the changes to the QA group. Although a specific QA engineer has not yet been assigned, a snapshot of the changes is made. The changes are copied into a *shadow work area*, which is a holding area for the changes. Each developer work area has a corresponding shadow work area. Because there is a strict pairing of a normal work area and its corresponding shadow work area, the changes that come from different developers working in different non-shadow work areas are kept separate from each other.

Shadow work areas are used because usually there are more content developers than QA engineers. Consequently, a change set can't be tested immediately upon completion. Therefore, the changes need to be held in a safe location until a QA engineer is ready to test. By mutual agreement, the shadow work areas hold the contents of handed-off contents. In particular, there is no direct editing of the content within a shadow work area by any developer or QA engineer. To do otherwise would break the convention that the shadow work area holds a snapshot of changes that have been handed off to QA, but for which a QA engineer has not yet been assigned.

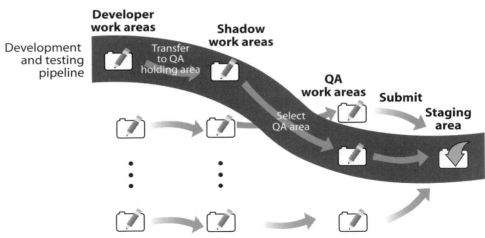

FIGURE B.2

Changes flow in a pipeline from development, through testing, to the staging area.

---

[1] Chapter 8, "Multiple Web Initiatives," describes in more detail an approach to allocating a task to a work area.

When a QA engineer takes ownership of the change list, then the files are copied from the shadow work area to a work area chosen by the QA engineer, which we refer to as the *QA work area*. The ability to choose the QA work area is useful because often there are only a limited number of QA work areas. For example, setting up a test setup for an application-server-based web site can be costly in hardware and software resources. Once the changes are in the QA work area, the web site can be put through its paces.

After testing, the QA engineer may approve the changes. Approval initiates the release procedure, which involves submitting the contents to the staging area, and releasing the changes to production. Alternatively, if the changes are rejected, the developer is notified by e-mail, and the job goes back to the beginning.

A detailed view of the flow of the changes from development is depicted in Figure B.3.

Changes are only made within developer work areas. This means that after the hand off and during the testing phase, no further changes are made. If additional changes need to be made, they are handled by resetting the workflow state back to the developer. After handing off the change set to QA, the content developer discontinues development on that change set; any subsequent changes would need to be overlaid

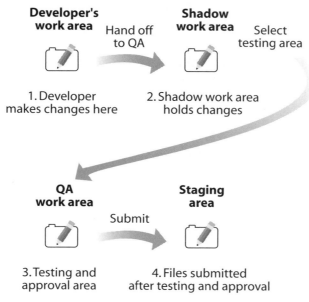

FIGURE B.3
Changes move through an approval pipeline.

on the changes already handed off to QA. By waiting for feedback from QA before making more changes, inconsistency and potential confusion are avoided.

On the QA side of the hand off, QA group is notified of the incoming job. Internally, the hand-off step makes a copy of the files identified in the change list. A member of the QA group sees the job, and takes ownership of the task. The QA engineer has one or more areas to test content. For example, if the content requires an application-server setup, there may be an area with a test instance of an application server. The QA engineer specifies a workarea for this purpose.

The QA engineer tests the files in the change list, and either approves or rejects the changes. On a rejection, the job state goes back to the content developer to revise the files. On an approval, the job transitions to a pre-production, and then to a production step. The completed job resides in an archived state.

Maintaining a fixed change set is essential for a good QA effort. If QA finds no errors or problems, then keeping the change set fixed means that the files are ready to proceed to the next step. On the other hand, if the set has changed, then at the minimum the additional changed files would need to be reexamined. Even worse, the known or potential interactions with the changes and the rest of the files could require that the QA effort start all over again.

Another reason to refrain from making more changes becomes evident in the event that QA finds a problem. Suppose the developer has further modified the files in question. This introduces confusion because the problem area could have changed or could even have vanished. In this eventuality, the effort by QA would be wasted since the subsequent changes negate the testing effort. Even if the QA engineer merely requests clarification about a particular aspect of the change set, allowing changes to occur just introduces unnecessary confusion. For similar reasons, it is important not to initiate another hand off from the same work area until approval is obtained.

Summary

This appendix illustrates how a workflow supports a formal hand-off procedure between a web development group and a QA group. In particular, it shows how a change set can be queued for anyone in the QA group to grab, thereby taking ownership of the task. The general technique is handy because the content developers usually outnumber the QA staff, and it would be impractical for the workflow to predetermine the particular QA engineer to handle the job.

A Workflow Design for Predetermined Time Schedules

Executive Summary

This workflow example shows how to support multiple web developers who have content to move into production on a predetermined time schedule. We show how this technique ensures that content scheduled for a particular time slot moves on schedule. Interactions between content from multiple sources that are scheduled for the same time slot are reviewed and tested together.

Problem Scenario

Denise works as a web producer at eportalzone.com. Next Monday she launches a 48-hour promotion for Star Trek collectibles. Star Trek memorabilia has become immensely popular with teens, and Denise anticipates that this will be the forerunner of many similar promotions. Denise has been working with a team of HTML, Shockwave, and MIDI developers on the new pages and associated web assets. She needs her content to go-live at the regular daily launch time of 11A.M. on Monday and to be torn down at the same time on Wednesday.

Denise's need for assets to be staged for production at a predetermined time, and her corresponding need to remove those assets at another predetermined time, is a common requirement. This is especially a requirement in e-businesses that have embraced the web as a vehicle of ongoing interactions with their customers.

continued

Meanwhile, another web producer, Lou, has obtained approval for a series of "teaser" announcements to commence on Monday, to support his upcoming rollout of a major cross-selling initiative between his company and a click-and-mortar company. Lou and the marketing communications group have developed a series of five ad banners that will run once each, starting Monday and extending through Friday.

Both Lou's and Denise's changes affect the homepage, and they need a solution that considers this interaction. Similarly, the solution needs to reflect that reviewers of the Wednesday content need to see both Lou's graphic and the expiration of Denise's 48-hour promotion in their proper contexts.

Background

In a typical WSE configuration, a work area corresponds to a project. For example, a web developer creates a new section of the web site. Perhaps she works with a graphic artist for new artwork. In this case, they are using a work area as a place to keep project-related changes. In another usage, a web producer makes corrections to a handful of web pages to fix factual inaccuracies or to avoid legal liability exposure. In this instance, the web producer uses the work area as a location to hold the changes associated with her project.

The project-based paradigm tends to be less appropriate when changes from different sources begin to overlap in terms of when they need to go-live. For example, if two web producers need to push out small changes to the homepage of a web site, it becomes cumbersome for each to maintain changes in their own work areas, and for one to merge the changes of the other after the other goes-live. This becomes even more cumbersome when the changes are completed in advance, and the two producers actually need to have their changes go-live at or near the same time. In this situation, having separate work areas is almost an artificial separation. The technique described here uses a work area in a different way, which applies in situations where changes overlap. This situation frequently arises when changes for a particular time slot are handled in batches.

Time-Slot Technique

The time-slot technique is used when content needs to be moved into production on a predetermined time schedule. Set up a work area to correspond to each window of time. For example, suppose a web site has assets that move daily and content is created up to a week in advance. Create five work areas, to correspond to Monday through Friday. If a web producer has a collection of assets for a promotion that will go-live on Monday, those assets are created and modified in a "Monday" work area. When Monday arrives, the modified files are submitted to the staging area. We refer to the Monday work area as the *primary* work area. (Usually this is done in force-overwrite mode.) Final checks and approvals are done, and the changes are deployed to production.

To make sure that changes in other work areas are performed on updated content after Monday's files are submitted, the other work areas—in this case, Tuesday through Friday—are updated in nonoverwrite mode. We refer to the other work areas, Tuesday–Friday, as secondary work areas. This means that all nonconflicting changes from the primary work area's submission are incorporated into the secondary work areas. For example, suppose that index.html and logo.gif are modified in the Monday work area. On Monday, these two files are submitted to staging. After the submit, the Tuesday work area is updated from staging. For the sake of argument, let's assume that Tuesday contains a modified index.html, but logo.gif is unmodified. When the nonoverwrite update is performed, the conflict on index.html prevents a change to index.html. On the other hand, there's no conflict with logo.gif, so it is updated in the Tuesday work area from the change submitted from the Monday work area.

The conflict between index.html in the Tuesday work area, and the index.html in the staging area from the Monday work area indicates that a decision needs to be made about the index.html in Tuesday. One possibility is that index.html in Tuesday ought to merge with index.html in the staging area. This is the right choice when at least some of the changes from Monday's index.html need to carry over into Tuesday's index.html. A second possibility is that one of the files supersedes the other, which might be the appropriate choice, for instance, if the index.html for Tuesday changes so drastically that it doesn't make sense to carry over the Monday changes.

Changes for other days are handled similarly. Changes for Tuesday go into Tuesday's work area, and so forth. When the day for a given work area arrives, the changes contained in that work area are submitted in force-overwrite mode to the staging area. Immediately following, all the other work areas are updated from staging in nonoverwrite mode.

Time-Slot Techniques—Detailed Example

Let's explore this technique in more detail. We'll focus on the sequence of events through a week. To keep things simple, let's assume that there are three sets of changes, possibly overlapping, being worked on by three web producers. Our story begins on Monday. At 9 A.M., Paula is tasked with making an emergency fix as soon as possible. Since Monday's daily push to production occurs at 11 A.M., Paula makes the fix in the Monday work area. Meanwhile, another web producer, Curt, commences work for his Friday promotion. He makes changes in the Friday work area. By 9:15 A.M., Paula's emergency change in the Monday work area is ready to be approved and submitted.

Paula obtains approval for her emergency changes. Her changes wait in the Monday work area. When the time to push to production arrives, Paula's changes, as well as changes from others, are submitted to the staging area.

Immediately after the Monday changes are submitted, the secondary work areas are updated in nonoverwrite mode with the changes from the staging area.

On Tuesday, another web producer, Liz, is assigned to prepare some changes to go-live on Wednesday. To recap, Curt's changes for Friday reside in the Friday work area, Liz's changes for Wednesday are held in the Wednesday work area. Paula's changes in the Monday work area have already moved into production.

Liz's changes are checked and approved within the Wednesday work area. By Wednesday, her changes are complete and are submitted to the staging area. See Figure C.1

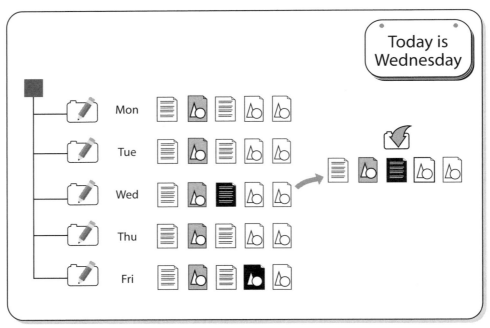

FIGURE C.1
Changes for Wednesday have gone to the staging area, ready for production.

As before, after the Wednesday work area has been submitted, the secondary work areas are updated from the staging area. This is shown in Figure C.2.

The update operation causes all nonconflicting changes to be pulled into the Monday, Tuesday, Thursday, and Friday work areas. In particular, Liz's nonconflicting changes are pulled into the Friday and Monday work areas in this manner. If they exist, conflicting changes from the Wednesday submission generate a warning to Curt and Paula, who may choose to merge changes, or not. Merging changes will resolve the conflict. If there are any remaining unresolved conflicts, their respective work area contents will overwrite the equivalent file in the staging area.

When Friday rolls around, Curt's changes in the Friday work area are submitted to the staging area in overwrite mode.

Let's summarize the time-slot technique.

Setup

1. Determine the greatest time between a change being initiated when it is going into production.

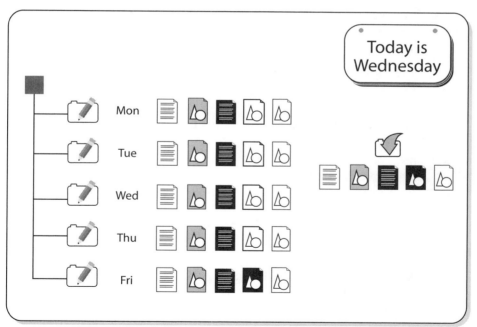

FIGURE C.2
Wednesday's changes propagate to the other work areas.

2. Create work areas to accommodate the daily changes based on the time span determined above.

3. Update each work area from staging.

Daily

1. Identify the work area that holds changes for today.

2. Overwrite-submit the changes to staging.

3. For each secondary work area the following happens.

 a. There is a nonoverwrite update from the staging area.

 b. Each remaining conflict generates a notification to the owner of the modified file for resolution.

Discussion

One of the benefits of the time-slot technique is that each developer works in the context of content that has gone live, because of the immediate update to the remaining work areas after a submit from the primary work area.

Use of the workareas is cyclic. Immediately after a work area has had its changes submitted, that work area can hold changes for the same day on the following week.

Notice how the conflicts, if any, between work area and staging area are handled at update time. The presence of a conflict indicates that the change in a secondary work area may need to be merged with the change submitted from the primary work area.

Variations on the Time-Slot Technique

This technique generalizes to many time slots. For example, we might have a daily time slice, and a seven-day cycle. In this case, we use seven work areas. Changes for an upcoming day of the week go into the work area corresponding to that day. As the work area for a given day comes due, the contents of that day's work area are submitted to staging (in overwrite mode). Subsequently, the other six work areas are updated with the contents of staging (in nonoverwrite mode). This cycle repeats each time slice, or daily, in this example.

There are many variations on this technique. First, work areas can be dynamically allocated. Second, changes in a work area can be "split" into two or more work areas as time granularity becomes finer as the work area due date approaches.

If a set of changes are being developed, but it is not yet known which predetermined time slot to apply the changes to, then those changes can be done in a different work area altogether. When the changes are ready, they can be copied to the appropriate work area.

If some changes are complete and approved, but that work area hasn't gone live yet, and the changes there are required for in-context work in days subsequent to it, they can be copied to the days that are in advance of it, but not beyond the current day.

BASIC PROCESS STEPS OF A BEST-PRACTICE CONTENT MANAGEMENT PROCESS

Executive Summary

It is common to have a web site that combines "classic" static web assets, HTML and GIF files, with web application code, as exemplified by Java servlets.[1] On most web sites, there are multiple web developers, each working on a different task simultaneously. We'll follow one member of a web development team as she uses the content management system to assist in the code development. We'll outline best-practice process steps that keep many developers working efficiently.

Example: Web Site

Figure D.1 shows a hypothetical externally visible web site for ezSuggestion-Box.com. Although this example shows only a handful of web assets, we should imagine that the actual production web site contains over 10,000 assets.

Figure D.2 shows the web site in development, with the changes that we need to make. In particular, three projects proceed concurrently:

1. ● Launch rebranding initiative.
2. ■ Launch OEM initiative.
3. ◆ Fix `signup.java` file.

---

[1] For more information, see Jason Hunter, *Java Servlet Programming*, O'Reilly & Associates, Sebastopol, CA, 1998.

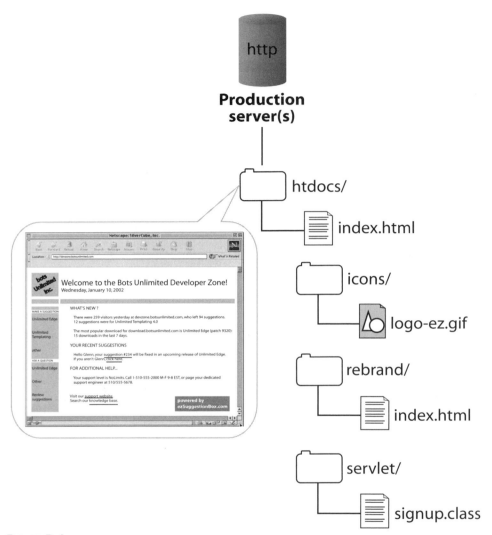

htdocs/

index.html

icons/

logo-ez.gif

rebrand/

index.html

servlet/

signup.class

FIGURE D.1
The ezSuggestionBox.com production web site combines Java servlets with "classic" HTML and GIF assets.

In the discussion below, we'll follow the changes that one of the web developers, Chris, will make. Chris is working on the rebranding initiative, whereby ezSuggestionBox.com rolls out the ability for partner companies to use EZSB's application service provider interface and to present a look-and-feel native to the partner company.

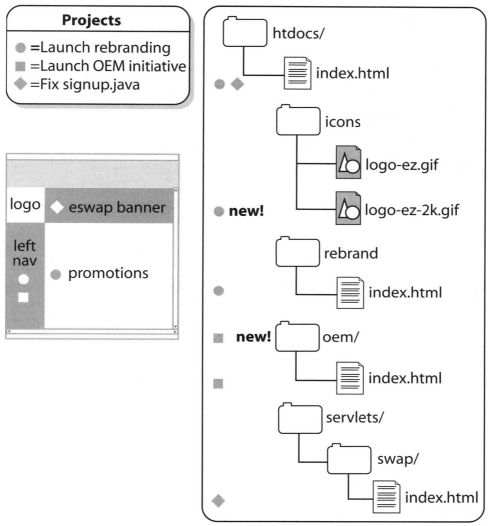

FIGURE D.2
The development group for the ezSuggestionBox.com web site has three pending tasks.

A Best-Practice Development Process

Let's walk though the development process for our hypothetical web developer, Chris. A web producer has assigned her a task. For the purpose of our discussion, we'll assume that she has a work area for her own use. This is the typical situation for a web developer making HTML or application code changes. She starts by comparing her work area with the contents of the staging area. Compare checks whether there are files that are in the staging area that we haven't updated into our work area. The most likely reason for such changes to exist is that someone else has submitted changes from another work area. If there are updates, then Chris brings those files into her work area, to ensure that her edits and testing are done on the latest contents in the staging area. If there are no updates, then Chris proceeds to make edits to complete her task. She tests her changes in her work area. If the changes don't work, or if the changes are not complete, she continues to edit. This cycle of edit-and-test is called the real-time development cycle. This cycle is important because all developers probably spend most of their time in this loop, making changes and testing changes.

When Chris is satisfied with her changes, she compares her work area against the staging area. If there are more recent files in the staging area, then Chris updates her work area or merges changes into her work area. Since changes have been made to her work area, Chris tests her work area again.

When Chris is satisfied with her changes and her work area is updated with the latest changes from the staging area, she finds someone to review her changes. The reviewer is often a peer. She shows the results of her changes to the reviewer. This is a useful process because a reviewer is often able to spot problems that the person making the changes has overlooked. In addition, the discipline of Chris describing the changes to another person helps her to think through her work. Sometimes she is able to find a problem just by taking time to talk through the rationale for her changes. At other times, the peer review process helps because it involves the reviewer with the changes; this can be helpful if someone is later called upon to make another change based on Chris's changes.

If the reviewer isn't satisfied, or if a problem is identified during the review, Chris makes the required modifications. This takes her back to the edit step. From the edit step, she repeats the cycle as before—testing, and then obtaining a review. Frequently, additional edit cycles are much shorter because changes identified in a review are less extensive than in the original edit. Often the reviewer will be satisfied with a verbal confirmation of the change, or may make a cursory check of the change. This cycle of edit-test-review is called the review cycle. This is the second most common cycle for a developer to spend time in.

When Chris's changes have been reviewed, and there are no required updates from the staging area, she submits her changes to the staging area. When she submits her files, she records comments documenting her work, why each file changed, and who reviewed her changes. The reviewer is acknowledged and thanked in the submit comments. The content management system triggers an automatic e-mail when the submit occurs, and Chris's group is sent a notification that certain files changed, together with the comments that she entered, together with the thank-you to the reviewer of Chris's changes.

This is a moment for celebration. Chris deserves to celebrate because she has tested her changes based on the latest contents of the staging area, she has made an effort to find a willing reviewer, and described her work to the reviewer. She has made sure that any latest changes in the staging area have been integrated with her changes.

The staging area collects changes from Chris as well as other developers. Since the other developers follow the same development process, we immediately see why the process works well. Each developer tests changes locally within his or her work area. On completion of this test, a peer review follows, updating and merging new changes in the staging area. It follows that all changes submitted to the staging area have the following properties. First, the changes have been tested against the latest changes in the staging area. Second, the changes have been peer reviewed. Third, the changes have been merged with any changes in the staging area.

By the development process described here, all changes are tested and reviewed. This greatly reduces the likelihood that a defect is able to slip undetected into the web site. In addition, because of the reviews, the development group members share a high level of awareness of the changes that have gone into the web site.

Example: Rebranding Initiative

Chris implements changes for the rebranding initiative. She begins by comparing her work area against the staging area to identify the latest changes in the staging area, shown in Figure D.3. This assures her that her changes are based on the latest content. In this example, someone else has submitted index.html and signup.java. Chris isn't surprised by these changes, because she had received e-mail notification when these changes were submitted.

Chris updates her work area with the changes from the staging area, shown in Figure D.4. Chris updates her work area to get the latest changes from the staging area. She pulls in `index.html` and `signup.java`. In this case, she knows that the changes that she is pulling in fix the problem with the Java implementation of the signup button on the homepage. A small handful of customers had reported that in some browsers the signup button didn't behave properly. This fixes that problem. Furthermore, she knows that these changes have already been tested and code reviewed, so she is confident that pulling in these changes won't introduce problems in her work area when it comes time to test her changes.

Knowing that her work area contains the latest changes, Chris proceeds to make her edits to implement the rebranding initiative. This is shown in Figure D.5. Chris changes `index.html`, adds a new GIF image for the logo, and introduces substantial changes to `rebrand/index.html`. We see that if she hadn't updated her work area before commencing her changes, there is a good chance that she would have made her changes to `htdocs/index.html` on something other than the latest version of that

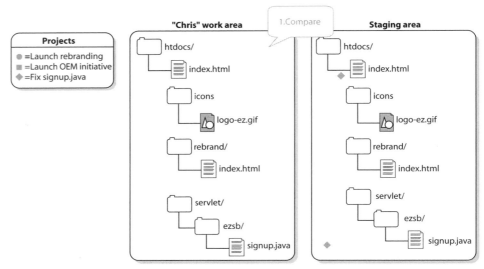

FIGURE D.3

Chris compares her work area against the staging area, which contains two files that have been submitted by another developer.

---

file. That would have required her to merge some time later. Worse, she might wind up clobbering the changes of the other developer.

After making the changes, Chris tests her changes, still keeping her modified files in her work area. This is shown in Figure D.6. By doing testing in her own work area, any problems that she introduces during her editing and testing don't affect others. Similarly, ongoing work by other developers doesn't affect Chris. This is the benefit of having separate work areas.

Chris tests her three files. When her changes look good to her, she solicits her colleague, Ted, to code review her changes. During the code review, Chris explains how the logic of her `index.html` page works, and how links to the rebranding subweb site work. She explains why the particular look of the gif file, `logi-ez-2k.gif`, was chosen. The code review helps Chris to recall aloud the discussions that led to the current state of her files. Ted is grateful to get Chris's explanation, because he knows that he may be called upon to make changes when Chris isn't available. Chris is thankful for the code review as well, because Ted sees a place in the `index.html` file where early versions of the Netscape browser have trouble with a certain usage of a JavaScript construct. He had recently fixed a problem elsewhere in the web site, so is happy to pass along his knowledge. Chris makes the change as Ted watches, and they both watch as they try out the new code on the older version of the browser.

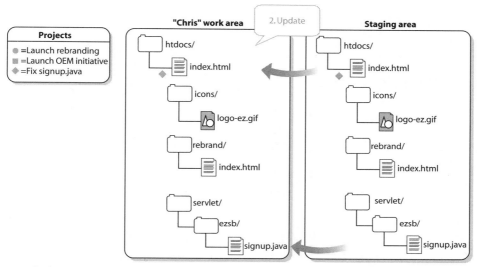

FIGURE D.4
Chris updates her work area to get the latest changes from the staging area.

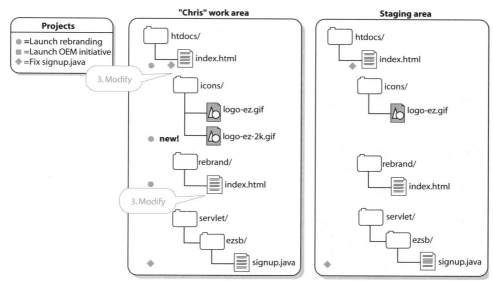

FIGURE D.5
Chris implements the changes required for the rebranding initiative.

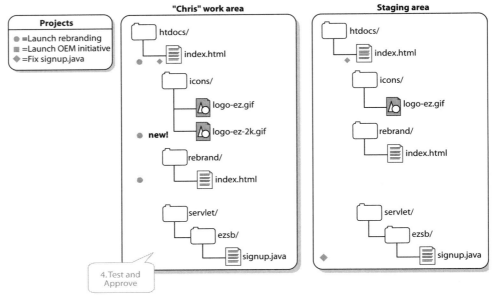

FIGURE D.6
After Chris is satisfied with her changes, she has a peer review her changes.

After getting the code review, and comparing her work area again against the staging area, Chris submits her changes to the staging area. Her submission comments explain the logic behind the links to the rebranding subweb site, and acknowledge Ted as the code reviewer. Because the submit action automatically triggers e-mail to Chris's group, everyone becomes aware that the rebranding subsystem has become functional. Moreover, they know that if they have questions, they can ask either Chris or Ted. This is shown in Figure D.7.

EzSuggestionBox.com has a practice of deploying a full copy of the staging area to a test server daily, for automated stress testing. If problems are detected, e-mail and pager notices are issued, and someone in the quality assurance group investigates. When the staging area is deemed good, an edition is published, and the contents are deployed during the evening to the web-server farm. If problems are detected on the deployment, email and pager notices are issued. This is shown in Figure D.8.

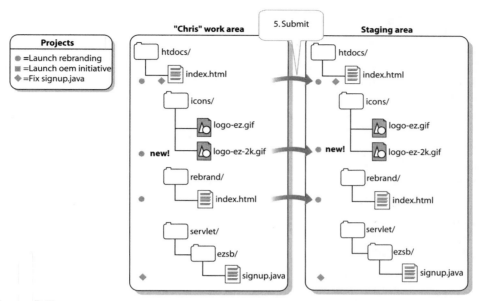

FIGURE D.7
After checking for more changes in the staging area, and finding none, Chris submits her changes to the staging area.

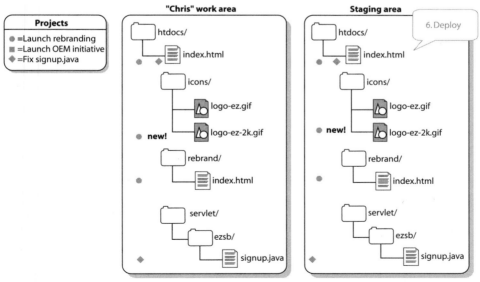

FIGURE D.8
After testing and review, the changes in the staging area are deployed to production.

Summary

In a best-practice web development process, there are four distinct testing cycles. Occurring most frequently is the real-time development cycle. This is where most developers spend the bulk of their time, editing and testing their changes. The next most frequent testing cycle is the compare and update cycle. Depending on how long a developer takes to make changes and test, other developers may have submitted changes that need to be pulled in.

The third most frequent cycle is the review cycle. When a developer is satisfied with her changes, she seeks a reviewer, typically a peer, to inspect and approve her changes. When the review is complete, the work area contains functioning, tested, and reviewed changes. At this point, the changes are submitted to the staging area.

The staging area collects submissions from many developers. On a regular basis, the staging area is tested. If the testing proves satisfactory, the contents of the staging area are deployed to production.

Resources

Bays, Michael E., *Software Release Methodology*, Prentice Hall PTR, Upper Saddle River, NJ, 1999.

Burdman, Jessica, *Collaborative Web Development: Strategies and Best Practices for Web Teams*, Addison-Wesley, Reading, MA, 1999.

Deitsch, Andrew and Czarnecki, David, *Java Internationalization*, O'Reilly, Sebastopol, California, 2001.

Koehler, Jerry W., et.al., *The Human Side of Intranets: Content, Style and Politics*, St. Lucie Press, Boca Raton, LA, 1998.

Marchand, Donald A. ed., *Competing with Information*, John Wiley & Sons, Ltd., Chichester, England, 2000.

O'Donnell, Sandra Martin, *Programming for the World: A Guide to Internationalization*, PTR Prentice-Hall, Upper Saddle River, NJ, 1994.

Tomsen, Mai-lan, *Killer Content: Strategies for Web Content and E-Commerce*, Addison-Wesley, Boston, MA, 2000.

White, Brian A., *Software Configuration Management Strategies and Rational ClearCase™: A Practical Introduction*, Addison-Wesley, Boston, MA, 2000.

INDEX

Also Available from Addison-Wesley

Collaborative Web Development
Strategies and Best Practices for Web Teams
Jessica Burdman

Today, Web site development requires the close collaboration of diverse professionals such as programmers, interactive designers and engineers, animators, videographers, writers, marketers, and businesspeople—all working within a highly coordinated and structured development process.

Written by a leader in Web development methodologies and processes, *Collaborative Web Development* brings structure and sanity to what is often an overwhelming and chaotic process. Drawing on the front-line experiences of practicing professionals and numerous real-world case studies, the author will help you get a handle on the issues and challenges you face, with proven strategies for effective coordination among team members and clients, a smooth development process, and a successful end result.

0-201-43331-1 • Paperback with CD-ROM • 272 pages • © 1999

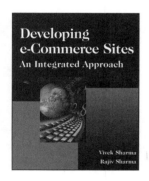

Developing e-Commerce Sites
An Integrated Approach
Vivek Sharma and Rajiv Sharma

This book leads you step-by-step through the process of building a sophisticated e-commerce Web site. It brings you up to speed on the latest technologies and shows you how to integrate them into a customized e-commerce site that serves your organization's specific needs. Details and instructions are reinforced by carefully crafted code examples that incorporate empowering technologies. The examples are included on the accompanying CD-ROM.

0-201-65764-3 • Paperback with CD-ROM • 640 pages • © 2000

e-Video
Producing Internet Video as Broadband Technologies Converge
H. Peter Alesso

As compression technology, streaming techniques, and transmission lines grow in efficiency, speed, and capacity, Internet video is fast becoming both viable and inevitable. This resource-packed guide to producing, encoding, editing, compressing, and serving video over the Internet lets you in on this coming "killer app." It presents the current tools and technologies that make Internet video possible and reveals likely future developments, allowing you to make knowledgeable investments in technology and equipment that anticipate these trends.

0-201-70314-9 • Paperback with CD-ROM • 304 pages • © 2000

Killer Content
Strategies for Web Content and E-Commerce
Mai-lan Tomsen
Addison-Wesley Information Technology Series

"This book is an excellent primer on competitive business strategies for providing value to your customer on the Web. If you're new to the world of e-commerce or looking to expand on an existing set of Web-based business strategies, this book is for you."

—*William T. Radcliffe, Director of Technology, Corbis*

A well-rounded guide for IT professionals and system architects, this book defines the changing models for Web-based commerce and shows you how to correlate the demands and rewards of digital commerce and adapt them to your own business environment. Killer Content explains this important value-added information for maintaining your content-driven business.

0-201-65786-4 • Paperback • 240 pages • © 2000

Web Engagement

Connecting to Customers in e-Business
Bill Zoellick
Addison-Wesley Information Technology Series

This book is the ideal introduction to understanding the key concepts necessary to engage, and ultimately retain, your Web customers. This book explains proven strategies that allow you to understand what your customers need and how you can use your Web site to meet those needs. Detailed case studies and examples illustrate what other Web businesses have tried—successfully and unsuccessfully—and what they have learned.

0-201-65766-X • Paperback • 224 pages • © 2000